D0081180

Evaluating Interpersonal Skills

in the Job Interview

Evaluating
Interpersonal Skills
in the Job Interview

A Guide for Human

Resource Professionals

JAMES B. WEITZUL

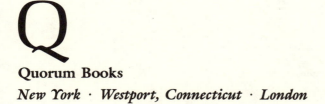

Quorum Books
New York · Westport, Connecticut · London

Library of Congress Cataloging-in-Publication Data

Weitzul, James B.
    Evaluating interpersonal skills in the job interview : a guide for
human resource professionals / James B. Weitzul.
      p. cm.
    Includes index.
    ISBN 0-89930-710-8 (alk. paper)
    1. Employment interviewing.   2. Personality and occupation.
3. Personality questionnaires. I. Title.
    HF5549.5.I6W456   1992
    658.3'1124—dc20   91-36293

British Library Cataloguing in Publication Data is available.

Copyright © 1992 by James B. Weitzul

All rights reserved. No portion of this book may be
reproduced, by any process or technique, without the
express written consent of the publisher.

Library of Congress Catalog Card Number: 91-36293
ISBN: 0-89930-710-8

First published in 1992

Quorum Books, One Madison Avenue, New York, NY 10010
An imprint of Greenwood Publishing Group, Inc.

Printed in the United States of America

∞™

The paper used in this book complies with the
Permanent Paper Standard issued by the National
Information Standards Organization (Z39.48-1984).

10 9 8 7 6 5 4 3 2 1

HF
5549.5
.I6
W456

1992

~~Con~~tents

Introduction

A number of books describe the steps necessary to conduct an employment interview sequentially, legally, and logically. Typically, these books describe a series of appropriate interview behaviors; list sensitive Equal Employment Opportunity Commission (EEOC) questions to avoid; include some techniques to define the position's skill requirements; list a series of questions designed to measure the candidate's technical knowledge to perform at a particular position; and recommend a set of questions to inquire about a person's interpersonal skills to perform these job requirements. These books are certainly helpful and provide a very useful function. This book, in many ways, begins where most of these other books end.

The book is designed to assist human resource professionals (or anyone who selects people to join a company) pick people where interpersonal skills are the most critical aspects of the job. Interpersonal skills are an increasingly important part of most management and sales job functions and can be critical at the senior management and sales management levels within an organization. These skills, however, are less important at the other end of the employment spectrum. Technical skill level may be the primary requirement for positions such as typists, secretarial staff, and some entry-level staff and administrative positions. At the managerial end of the job spectrum, however, where dealing with people and achieving results through, with, and by others is a critical talent, interpersonal skills are critical to success in the position. This book is designed to assist you evaluate a candidate's suitability for employment with your organization, with particular emphasis on the candidate's interpersonal skills as they relate to the position requirements.

Each chapter builds sequentially so that a reasonable knowledge of each chapter is helpful in understanding the next one. Obviously, topics in advanced math are not being explored here, so experienced interviewers can skip among the chapters; however, it is recommended that you at least page through the chapters successively before skip-reading through the book. Some chapters, because of their titles, may appear more interesting than others, but, again, it is recommended that you review the chapters sequentially at least once. For your convenience and interest, each chapter is described briefly here.

Chapter 1 introduces the book and lays a broad foundation for the main topics discussed throughout the volume. It establishes the book's primary focus and defines the boundaries of the material presented here. Initially, the importance of determining the interpersonal skills required by a given position is clearly stated. Then the focus of the book—measuring the candidate's interpersonal skills as required by the position—is introduced. Next, the chapter mentions the idea of describing candidates in terms of their behavior traits and suggests that this approach to categorizing people is the cornerstone of understanding the candidates' interpersonal skills. Finally, the chapter introduces the 120, 220, and 320 questionnaires, which are used to measure a person's behavior style and define his interpersonal skills.

Chapter 2 lays additional groundwork for determining the candidate's interpersonal skills. The first step is to understand the seven behavior traits that are the basis for categorizing behavior. The reader needs to accept that most behavior can be categorized into these seven traits. This acceptance is a large but necessary step in digesting the material presented here; that is, it is necessary to understand the traits described and to agree that they adequately define a large portion of behavior. Next, the idea of a person's behavior style is introduced. A person's behavior style is defined as the combination of a person's separate traits into an overall behavior pattern. For example, most people will demonstrate behavior typical of two or three traits. The resulting behavior, which is representative of the interaction of these traits, is referred to as a person's behavior style.

Chapter 3 serves two purposes. First, it introduces the 120 Questionnaire, which is contained in appendix A. This form is used as a generic application blank. It requests information from the candidate on such topics as education, work experience, job history, and positions liked and disliked. It then explores specific work situations in more depth by asking questions about favorite supervisors, companies, and work environments. It requests information about conflict situations, future goals, and long-term aspirations. Next, candidates are asked to rank order a series of work-related goals. This questionnaire concludes with a section of sentence completion exercises. In this section the candidate is asked to complete a number of phrases such as "When working with others."

The second purpose of this chapter is a detailed explanation of the 120 Questionnaire. It examines the questions in detail, provides some rationale for asking them, and helps the interviewer interpret the responses. It accomplishes this purpose by examining responses from individuals whose actual behavior typified one of the behavior traits defined in chapter 2. With this information the interviewer can begin to draw inferences about the candidate's probable behavior style. The 120 Questionnaire is, however, only the first step in the interviewing process.

Chapter 4 recounts the importance of preparing for the interview. The importance of this apparently simple step is easy to overlook, with possibly grave consequences. The costs of an inadvertent remark or an inappropriate hire or, conversely, of overlooking solid talent are high. Hence, this chapter is important unto itself, and it also lays the groundwork for discussing the interview process itself.

Chapter 5 reviews some thoughts and procedures to maximize the successful outcome of the interview. A basic tenet of this chapter is to remind the interviewer to put himself in the position of the interviewee, that is, the interviewer needs to help the candidate relax and tell his story. One of the best ways to achieve this goal is with open-ended questions and appropriate reinforcement. At the same time, the interviewer needs to control the interview politely and direct the conversation to the areas that interest him by clarifying any confusing or contradictory statements and focusing on the facts of the interviewee's life story and the behaviors he uses to convey those facts.

First, chapter 6 builds on the lessons reviewed during the discussion of the interview process. It lists and defines some topic areas and, using the 220 Questionnaire, which is contained in appendix B, it presents specific questions to ask during the interview. The questions probe the candidate's abilities over a generic set of managerial talents and represent refinements of earlier sets of questions that have been asked and are now succinctly boiled down to a critical essence. Hence, the questions do not include the somewhat shopworn standards like "What are your strengths?" and "What are your weaknesses?" The questions listed have been carefully selected to enable the interviewer to gauge the candidate's responses and gain additional insight about his behavior style.

Second, this chapter guides the interviewer through the candidate's responses to the questions. Much as chapter 3 was a guidebook for interpreting the candidate's background, this chapter becomes a yardstick for interpreting the candidate's verbal responses during the interview. This chapter describes how patterns of responses can be interpreted and also used to define the candidate's behavior traits/style. The interviewer gains a firmer impression of "what makes the candidate tick" and begins to firm up some impressions about the candidate's suitability for the position.

Chapter 7 is the final integration of the preceding material. If the process has been followed carefully, this final interpretation is simply the next step in the process of the interview. At each step, facts, opinions, and observations regarding the appropriateness of the candidate have been considered. These individual data points have either been incorporated into your overall impression of the candidate or been systematically discarded. The final decision about the person is merely the accumulation of the individual decisions that you have already made about him; the final interpretation should be comparatively easy.

Admittedly, the final integration is part science, based on your observations, and part art, based on your intuitive judgment about those facts. You have sufficient tools, however, to discern the candidate's abilities in a number of areas, including problem solving, planning and organizing, social aggressiveness, money motivation, and so on. From these individual assessments of the person, you should be able to define the individual reasonably well and generally determine his behavior style.

Finally, the chapter provides a quick summary of the ideas expressed in the previous chapters and reviews the value of using the 120 and 220 questionnaires for an accurate definition of a candidate for a position. It also offers an additional option: If you still feel uncomfortable with your decision or want a second opinion about a person, the 320 Questionnaire is defined, and a mail-in procedure is described to allow you to gain that additional opinion.

The Approach:
The Interviewing Mind-set

This chapter sets the parameters of the book by defining the limits and boundaries of what will be discussed in the remainder of the text. This purpose is important because, for example, the book does not dwell on the steps necessary to perform a complete job analysis, nor does it emphasize the importance of EEOC considerations in the selection decision. The book acknowledges that both of these topics are important and worthy of detailed attention, but they are not the primary focus.

A quick read of this chapter will readily set the stage for the remainder of the material. From the information contained here, you should begin to develop a certain approach to reviewing information about job candidates; that is, this chapter is intended to convey the need to develop a certain mind-set as part of the interviewing process, rather than to convey a set of facts per se.

The chapter focuses on the importance of understanding the concept of behavior traits/behavior styles and introduces the reader to a series of specific traits that will be repeatedly referenced throughout the book. You should gain a preliminary understanding of the idea of these behavior traits. Moreover, you will acquire some feeling for the idea of categorizing people's behavior into these traits. Finally, you should mentally begin to see that everything a candidate writes, says, or communicates during the entire interview process has some meaning and can be indicative of some underlying behavior trait.

IMPORTANCE OF EFFECTIVE INTERVIEWING

The search for the right man or woman for the job can be a long and arduous process and, sadly, often becomes one of simple trial and error. To take some of the error out of the employee search, this book includes information on general interviewing techniques and specific information on how to measure a candidate's interpersonal skills so that these skills can be compared with those required for a particular position.

The interviewer is taught to interpret historical behavior patterns as well as the candidate's interview responses. Moreover, the book shows how to interpret this information and form impressions about an individual's specific behavior traits and overall behavior style. In essence, the book is designed to assist you to interview candidates for a broad range of interpersonal skills that are related to success in a variety of positions. This measurement of interpersonal skills is perhaps most important in positions requiring managerial and/or sales skills.

Interviewing is a serious responsibility. The cost of incorrect hires is two-fold: First, the process is expensive and second, if the wrong person has been selected and the right one screened out, then additional expense will be incurred. Interviewing is both an art and a science. One is expected to glean not only information such as level of experience but also information about interpersonal skills that will make or break the employee in the job situation. These are often the most difficult to explore. There is no formula for finding the interpersonal strengths and weaknesses of an individual, but through careful planning and questioning the interviewer becomes much more effective at controlling the interview and at making a valid assessment of an individual's interpersonal skills.

In the preliminary stages of the employee search it becomes essential to determine what the position calls for, in terms not only of actual skills but of experience and background. The employer must consider the future needs of the department or position for which he is interviewing, as well as the everyday concerns of the job. An individual who can get along well with people may not be the individual who will eventually manage his department. In the same light, an individual who is aggressive and successful in individual sales may not have the interpersonal skills to manage a regional sales force.

DEVELOPING A POSITION DESCRIPTION

Many interviewing books emphasize the importance of carefully defining the requirements of a given position. Thus, developing a position description is sometimes incorporated in the interviewing process. This volume readily acknowledges the importance of defining the position requirements but does not include a technical discussion of the mechanics of performing this task. The overall process of defining a position's requirements is traditionally referred to as developing a SKAP profile. Indeed, it is the interviewer's responsibility to know the different combinations of skills, knowledge, abilities, and personal characteristics needed to fill a position. The necessity for conducting some form of SKAP profile is discussed briefly in chapter 5.

FOCUSING ON INTERPERSONAL SKILLS

This book enables the interviewer to categorize that portion of the candidate's skill, knowledge, abilities, and personal characteristics that relates to human interaction in terms of a single category. This single category is described as the interpersonal skills that are required for a given position.

Moreover, this book is designed to help managers understand the personal dynamics of each person that they interview. For example, is the candidate a competitive individualist or a team player? Is he motivated more by money or by organizational perks? Does he see value in developing long-term relationships, or does he simply focus on the immediate task?

The book is designed to assist the interviewer to understand the candidate as a whole person. How is the person likely to be on the job? Will he react favorably to pressure? How will he interact with the other members of the organization in terms of complementing them, as required by the position? Will they effectively work together as required? Will the candidate make a meaningful contribution within the existing organizational atmosphere?

In essence, the book is designed to help the interviewer understand and define the candidate as an individual. We are all different, with unique habits and traits, but at the same time we each possess characteristics that can be measured and recorded. Educational attainment, work history, and present income can be reviewed and evaluated. These factors allow us to make approximate groupings of people. Equally important measurements can be taken of factors like social aggressiveness, money motivation, and team spirit.

We are interested in recording this information because it can be used to form meaningful categories. By measuring and combining these separate pieces of information about a person, we can form a picture of the total individual and make predictions about his interpersonal skill level. This skill level can be compared to the position requirements to make a valid selection decision.

BEHAVIOR TRAITS/BEHAVIOR STYLES

The methods used here to measure an individual's interpersonal skills are initially based on an understanding of seven behavior traits. The traits can be used alone or in combination to understand a candidate's interpersonal skills. When analyzed singly, they are referred to as a candidate's behavior traits; when individual traits are combined, they are referred to as a candidate's behavior style.

Individual interpersonal skills can be very specific and therefore difficult to measure in an interview situation. The behavior traits, however, are generally broader-based trait patterns involving a collection of individual skills. For this reason, they are generally easier to determine during the interview.

Thus, while it may be difficult to decide if a person possesses a certain interpersonal skill, it will be much easier to determine if he possesses a behavior trait. If he possesses a given trait, then he most likely possesses the interpersonal skills associated with that trait. So, the first step in defining a person's specific set of interpersonal skills is to determine his individual behavior traits. The seven behavior traits are:

- overachiever
- entrepreneur
- active
- passive
- sensitized
- aggressive
- compulsive

A person's behavior trait refers to one of these categories. A person's behavior style refers to the combination of these traits, the candidate's whole motivational structure. These motives may appear different to different people, but each person will demonstrate a relatively consistent manner of interacting with his social environment. Once this manner is understood, a particular person's behavior style becomes highly predictable in a work situation. Moreover, once we understand a candidate's behavior style, we are better prepared to determine if that person's style will fit into the position requirements of the organization.

The next chapter defines these behavior traits and behavior styles with more explicit and complete definitions. The interviewer then gets a general idea of what some behavior traits will mean to job performance and interpersonal skills. Once the employer recognizes hints of behavior traits in the candidate's application, he may further explore their implications in the interview.

MEASUREMENT OF THE BEHAVIOR TRAITS

Three questionnaires are used to define the candidate's behavior traits and predict his interpersonal skills: 120 Questionnaire (application blank), 220 Questionnaire (interviewer questions), and 320 Questionnaire (temperament survey). Together they are called the behavior profile.

The 120 Questionnaire, presented in appendix A, gives the interviewer a thorough picture of the candidate's biographical history. An elongated application blank, it is composed of approximately 120 questions about an individual's education, work experience, preferred work positions, supervisors, and environments. The questionnaire was designed by psychologists to explore many areas of the individual's background and past experience.

The candidate's responses provide the interviewer insights into the candidate's behavior traits by reviewing and elaborating on his biographical record. The candidate is asked to reveal feelings unique to certain situations at work. The information gained from this questionnaire is crucial as the preliminary step toward more effective interviewing. As patterns develop in written response to the 120 Questionnaire, the book affords the interviewer information essential to exploring these patterns in detail; this information results from using the 220 Questionnaire.

The 220 Questionnaire, in appendix B, is an optional list of questions to be asked by the interviewer. It is composed of approximately 220 questions and covers a set of specific areas. The responses to these questions can be used as a guideline throughout the interview to explore levels of personal attributes such as drive, self-image, and self-development, as well as stress tolerance, adaptability, and persuasiveness.

Many interviewing books include sample questionnaires similar to the 120 and 220 questionnaires. This book, however, also provides actual responses from individuals whose behavior patterns were categorized into the seven behavior traits listed above; that is, the book includes sample responses to the 120 and 220 questionnaires by individuals whose actual behavior typified the different behavior traits/styles. Further, an analysis of the responses is provided so that the interviewer will be able both to effectively code and to interpret the responses he receives from a given candidate. In this way, it is possible to compare the responses each candidate provides in the 120 Questionnaire and to the 220 Questionnaire with responses of individuals with known behavior traits/styles.

To enhance the interview further, chapters on the interview preparation and process are included. This information will enable the interviewer to determine a candidate's behavior traits and his interpersonal skills. Finally, the candidate's interpersonal skills can be compared to the position requirements as developed in the SKAP profile.

One final step in the candidate evaluation is the 320 Questionnaire, presented in appendix C. This optional questionnaire is composed of 320 statements that the candidate answers either yes or no. The answer sheet is then forwarded for additional analysis (see Appendix C). The analysis of the 320 Questionnaire can double-check and/or fine-tune the impressions gained by using the 120 and 220 questionnaires.

CONCLUSION

This book provides the skills necessary to interview people and to define their behavior traits/styles. This knowledge will enable you to make better decisions about two key items about your candidates: if they possess the interpersonal skills (drive, initiative, self-discipline, and effective communication) needed to be effective in the proposed position, and if they possess the skills to be effective in dealing with the interpersonal responsibilities of a managerial, sales, or sales management position.

2

Seven Behavior Traits

A thorough knowledge of the ideas expressed in this chapter forms the basis for the remainder of the book. The ideas presented here are fairly simple and easy to understand. There are no complex formulas involved nor abstract reasoning required; in some ways, the ideas are nothing more than straight common sense. Once you gain a feeling for the ideas expressed here, you will have the building blocks for understanding the material that follows.

This chapter presents a simple set of ideas for describing human behavior. Human behavior is diverse and complex. Each of us is unique, different, and separate from any other person. At the same time, we readily exhibit characteristics and traits that allow us to be categorized into certain groups. As an example, distinct differences can be described in terms of common employment position requirements. That is, some positions require a license to sell stocks and bonds, others may need the qualifications of a certified public accountant, while still others require a medical degree. So, people with the qualifications for each of these position requirements can be easily categorized. Certainly, some overlap exists in that a C.P.A. may also hold a license to sell securities. But generally speaking, in categorizing individuals for employment, people can be divided into one of a number of distinct groups.

In the same way, an individual's behavior traits can be defined and categorized. The categorization process may not be as carefully defined as that of a C.P.A. or medical doctor. Some definitions, however, can still be given to an individual's behavior traits that will enable them to be distinguished from another person's behavior traits. This book indicates that behavior can be categorized into seven specific behavior traits and that these traits can be combined, for an individual, into a total pattern referred to as a behavior style.

Most people feel comfortable with the idea that every person is unique, singular, and different in ways that are special to him, and this idea is certainly true. At the same time, however, science is based on the idea of being able to define and categorize objects with meaningful and reliable labels. For example, physical science deals with materials that are liquid, solid, and/or gaseous. In the same way, some branches of social science categorize people as populations, cultures, and/or groups. In general, psychology deals with individuals. Moreover, the usefulness and practicality of describing individuals by using behavioral traits have a long and scientific tradition within the practice of psychology.

The terms *introvert* and *extrovert* are based on the theories of Dr. Carl Jung. Other psychological theorists have listed and defined a number of behavior traits that describe human behavior. The seven traits used here come from that same tradition. These traits are intended to be used as categories to enhance your understanding of people as individuals. It is not the intention to foster or encourage the use of stereotypes, but the use of types per se can be and is a useful and practical way to begin to type the general behavior patterns of people. Once a person is generally typed, it is much easier to understand the general behavioral trends that compose his unique personality. A better understanding of the traits can be gained by a quick review of the research that led to their development.

In the research, a series of generic traits was listed and defined. The traits were chosen to represent different aspects of the typical behavior of normal people in living their daily lives. The composition of the initial list was the result of an extensive literature search of the professional journals in psychology. From this search, a list of generic traits was decided upon. This original trait list was composed of over 100 traits. Additional research was completed, and this list was condensed into seven traits.

The next step of the project focused on identifying individuals whose actual life history behavior patterns exemplified the seven behavior traits. In this way, individuals were classified, based on their everyday behavior patterns and life histories, as belonging to certain life-history-trait-groups. An individual was assigned to these groups when and if two psychologists independently agreed that the individual's life history was representative of a specific trait. So, seven groups of individuals were formed. Each individual in each group was selected for a group on the basis of his life history. This life history reflected behavior indicative of one of the seven traits.

This categorization process was accomplished by reviewing the individual's personal background, education, work history, and life experiences for evidence of a specific trait. Individuals whose life history indicated the presence of a particular trait were then independently interviewed by two psychologists. If the information learned in the interviews confirmed the information reviewed in the analysis of the person's life history—that is, that the person's life history was indicative of a given trait—then the person was given an additional interview.

The purpose of this further interview was to further understand the person's traits. If the person exhibited traits (in terms of explaining his life situations) consistent with the behavior trait suggested by the review of his life history, then the person was considered to possess a temperament representative of that trait. For example, some people, because of their life histories, were tentatively identified as possessing a large amount of the entrepreneurial trait. If these people confirmed the possession of this entrepreneurial trait during the interviews, then they were considered to be representative of the entrepreneurial person. This confirmation meant that they indicated a high degree of interest in money, generally showed competitive behavior, were prone to risk taking, and were diplomatically persuasive, clever, and interested in advancing their own cause.

Only individuals with definable patterns of life history, who also verified aspects of the trait during separate interviews, were defined as possessing temperaments representative of a given trait. If a person was not consistently rated in both the review of his life history and the interviews as being representative of a certain trait, then he was eliminated from this portion of the study.

The life history and interview questionnaires used in this process were developed into the 120, 220, and 320 questionnaires. In this way the 120, 220, and 320 questionnaires were validated on individuals whose actual life patterns reflected the seven traits.

A statistical analysis of the results of the questionnaires completed by people with different life histories revealed that these individuals (whose life patterns partially reflected a mirror image of each trait) responded to the questionnaires with statistically unique patterns.

For example, individuals whose life pattern suggested primarily a high component of the overachiever trait responded to the 120, 220, and 320 questionnaires in a manner statistically different from individuals who were categorized as possessing primarily a high degree of each of the other traits. This same type of analysis was completed for the remainder of the behavior traits. Further, this same general process was followed for individuals whose behavior was considered to be primarily two or three traits.

The responses to the 120 and 220 questionnaires by individuals in each of the trait groups were analyzed using a technique referred to as content analysis.

The responses to the 320 Questionnaire were analyzed using a series of statistical programs, including analysis of variance, multiple regression, and factor analysis. The results of these analyses enabled the researcher to define the seven traits and behavior styles more carefully.

For example, part of the population studied for defining some of the aspects of the overachiever traits were individuals who had achieved positions of importance far beyond what might otherwise be expected, given their circumstances. In particular, some adults whose parents had died at an early age, who possessed average intelligence, and who received little financial support from other family members—but who also completed college degrees and attained positions of importance in business, government, or academia sooner than would be expected, given their age—were included in the study. If they appeared to achieve their relatively exalted position based primarily on their own self-discipline, they were defined as overachievers.

The list serves as a useful starting point to describe and define an individual's interpersonal skills. Consider the traits as a set of building blocks that can be arranged and grouped to define a person's collection of behavior traits. Individuals can be defined as possessing primarily one or more traits. The behavior of most people suggests that they can best be described by two or three traits. In this instance, where two or three traits are used to describe a person's behavior, the phrase *behavior style* is used to define the person's trait pattern.

This brief review is not intended to answer all the questions a person may raise concerning the development of the traits; however, it is designed to provide a brief overview of the process. Indeed, these seven traits and the combined behavior styles described are the result of years of research. For example, once the traits were defined as representative of actual behavior, additional long-term studies were performed to show how different amounts of the traits are associated with success in a variety of sales occupations, and the questionnaires have been used to predict success in sales positions. A complete description of the research steps undertaken and the studies involved to design, construct, and validate the types is available from the author.

OVERACHIEVER

The overachiever is typified by a single-minded dedication to the goal of self-improvement. He measures himself constantly in an attempt to uncover any weakness and rigidly disciplines himself to correct even the slightest perceptible fault. Like the research chemist in the laboratory who carefully measures scientific relationships and controlled reactions, the overachiever works at measuring himself and his behavior in innumerable, different situations so that he can better understand and validly measure his capacity for improvement. Self-improvement becomes an end in itself for him by practicing discipline and control of his emotions. At the same time that he is striving to correct what he may see as a fault, he also seeks out additional work or social responsibilities to expand his level of ability.

Hence, he may be perceived as a finely tuned balance, restricting himself with almost rigid self-discipline on the one hand and constantly striving for increased control of his environment on the other. The Olympic decathlon competitor perhaps optimally describes the overachieving individual, constantly measuring and checking himself for imperfection to improve his ability as compared to ever-increasing standards of performance. Much as the decathlon competitor will run for hours on a sandy beach to improve his overall performance, the overachiever will run his mind over figures to understand better a balance sheet, a chemical reaction, or an inventory problem of a few missing widgets.

Overachievement is an attitude independent of natural ability and in many situations will catapult the individual with moderate ability much higher than would ordinarily have been predicted. The overachiever possesses the constant persistence of the small train saying, "I can do it, I can do it, I can do it"; he personifies the attitude of the lightweight guard who gobbles bananas prior to weigh-in just to qualify for tryouts on the varsity football team; he embodies the virtue of the individual who looks himself in the mirror and honestly reports, "I'm not much, but I'm all I've got, so I'm going to do my best with what I have."

The degree to which a person possesses this controlled discipline and sees himself as master of his own fate is certainly definable as a single force, but it also directly affects the individual's entire behavior style. This single trait interacts with, controls the limits of, and dominates the influence of the other traits in the person's actual behavior pattern.

This trait plays a master control role in the direction of the other traits and may be compared to the brain of the human body. If a person possesses a superior brain, then he is capable of superior achievement; he will not necessarily attain it, but he is certainly capable of reaching great heights. If the person's brain function has been seriously impaired, however, then under the best of conditions he can reach only certain levels of performance. In much the same way, the presence of the overachieving orientation is associated with but does not necessarily cause achievement in real life. The lack of this attribute, however, will limit a person's control of the other traits of his temperament and will ultimately limit his overall effectiveness.

"When the going gets tough, the tough get going" would be a typical statement of the overachiever. He delights in volunteering for assignments simply to see if he is capable of performing up to the standards required. Fictional characters like Tarzan, the Lone Ranger, Zorro, Wonder Woman, and Flash Gordon typify this orientation of self-mastery, discipline, and control and have served as models for more than one developing overachiever. He listens to rational, logical discussions about a certain problem but finds it almost impossible to lower his own standards of performance or accept less than 100 percent effort from people associated with him on a task. This perfectionistic approach to problem solving can prove a source of real irritation to people who work for the overachiever.

The overachiever tends to be emotional in a rational way; that is, he will control his feelings. He will utilize his emotions in a constructive manner. Emotions are seen by the overachiever as a kind of energy that he can harness and put to work. For example, if the overachiever is angry at someone in the work situation, he may put his feelings to work by striving that much harder to find a solution to the problem he is working on, or he may use the anger in a constructive way to deal with the person who made him angry. He may strive to come up with some agreement with the other person to minimize the friction between them. The overachiever can be thought of as someone who will use all of his resources, including his emotional energy, to achieve his goals in a rational way. The overachiever is not a basically cold person, but someone who believes that emotion, like everything else in life, should be used in a rational manner.

Someone who is a moderate overachiever will have the discipline to concentrate fully and to complete a task when necessary but will also have the ability to relax and enjoy himself in social situations. A moderate overachiever is, to a considerable extent, self-disciplined and regulated but is more sociable and better adept at functioning with people than is the high overachiever.

A low overachiever is essentially a prisoner of his own impulses; he is irresponsible and unable to maintain relationships over long periods. "Here today, gone tomorrow" describes this person. Although perhaps likable because of his readiness to try anything, he is frequently undependable.

In general, the overachiever may be described as the person who

1. uses his own standards to measure himself and others,
2. can sometimes appear cold as he strives for self-control,
3. is efficient in the expenditure of his energy,
4. is relentless in his pursuit of excellence and the high goals he sets for himself,
5. may appear somewhat austere, determined, and socially formal, although he means well,
6. endeavors always to view things rationally and unemotionally,
7. works for self-improvement and is critical of his own shortcomings,
8. generally is conservative with his resources,
9. shows little emotion and keeps his reactions under control, and
10. is conscientious about following social rules.

ENTREPRENEUR

In the previous section, the overachiever was described as a person whose prime motivations of self-discipline, control, and almost puritanical conservatism became ends in themselves and guidelines for the increased levels of responsibility he could meaningfully accept. The overachiever is not always loved due to perfectionistic standards, but he is readily respected for his objective, unbiased appraisal of situations as well as his desire to lead with an emphasis on demonstration, not just instruction.

The entrepreneur behavior trait is in sharp contrast to this study in self-imposed rigidity. The entrepreneur is competitive and eager to win; he may appear vain and proud of his accomplishments. He tends to be clever in business negotiations and somewhat shrewd in his attempts to achieve his goals of material gain and financial independence. He is very insightful in reading people and capable of quickly modifying his own social demeanor to gain acceptance by others. In brief, the "pure" entrepreneur may be thought of as 50 percent Yankee trader and 50 percent southern gentleman but is 100 percent for himself.

The entrepreneur is competitive, ambitious, money-motivated, and eager for individual recognition for his contribution to any group effort. He is interested in self-improvement, but his interpretation of this phrase tends to emphasize self, and his idea of improvement is typically measured in dollars and status. His orientation and goals are related primarily to material gain so that he may live in conspicuous comfort and comparative luxury. In essence, for him, gaining physical possessions is a measure of success and self-worth. He tends to focus his energies on the accomplishment of the goal of having more. Hence, his occupation, his personal relationships, and even his outside interests are channeled into gaining him greater financial independence.

Although the entrepreneur is typically self-centered, he also extends this shield of preservation to his immediate family. He sees family members as an extension of himself, and he can become incredibly disciplined and focused when any form of financial danger approaches his family. Under pressure for family self-preservation, he can draw on unused energy reserves to exculpate himself and family from a dangerous situation. If successful in this endeavor, however, he is inclined to tempt fate a second time with his own behavior. That is, having overcome and been rewarded for escaping one set of impossible circumstances, he delights in flirting with fate again, ultimately to his own downfall. At such times he is likely to remark, "Well, my luck just ran out."

The entrepreneur will typically show more vanity than will the average person. Moreover, he enjoys showing off his possessions and achievements. In his ambition to "keep up with the Joneses," however, he sometimes stretches himself too thin. For example, he may fault his new Mercedes as being too expensive to drive and repair, although he will frequently mention owning it. He delights in having people marvel at his trophies, awards, and indications of social/business accomplishment. In all fairness, he will have legitimately won the awards, but he is generally more impressed with the plaques of success than are the members of his audience.

This vanity can cause the entrepreneur to work harder at his responsibilities, in the sense of appealing to his competitive energies. But the resulting arrogance, if he is successful, can have a negative effect on other members of the work group. Young, immature, or otherwise impressionable employees in the organization may find the assumed or rumored exploits of the entrepreneur fascinating and great material for office gossip.

The entrepreneur possesses a highly refined sense of money. He is frequently regarded as a shrewd and capable businessperson. True enough, he is more than able to analyze, interpret, and act upon information that may affect him financially. The characters Rhett Butler and Scarlett O'Hara in the novel *Gone with the Wind* portrayed evidence of entrepreneurial traits. Both were sociable but somewhat conceited, polished but generally self-serving, and they were money-motivated. At the same time, both characters were goal-motivated and eager to achieve their objectives, almost at any cost.

"All I need is a good angle" is a frequently expressed concern of the entrepreneur. He possesses an uncanny belief that the "big strike" is just around the corner. Moreover, when it comes to risk taking and advancement based largely on chance, the entrepreneur is a heavy player. If by chance his long shot should pay off, he sees himself as a highly skilled businessperson; but, if the risk taking follows normal probability curves, he will indicate that he is "suffering from a string of bad luck." Of course, certain exceptions exist, and a moderate degree of risk taking is certainly an asset to an individual in an organization. Oftentimes it is a means of attracting the boss's attention and increasing one's mobility from the mail room to the boardroom.

Part of the entrepreneur's interest in personal material gain is a need for acceptance into high social groups. The entrepreneur is interested in working toward goals that include gaining social status. For example, being perceived as a person who gives freely to social causes can raise his social level in some circles. Part of the reason for the entrepreneur's shrewdness and interest in manipulation is to obtain socially approved goals. Unlike, however, the persons with active and passive behavior traits (as discussed in the next two sections), who tend to respond emotionally to many situations, the entrepreneur will use his emotions in a controlled manner to enhance his personal gain. In social situations, where members of an appealing social group are present, he can be expected to put on quite a show of team effort and goodwill for the cause.

The behavior of the entrepreneur is both similar to and different from that of the overachiever. He is similar in that he is primarily concerned with himself, but he is very different in that he tends to use more immediate means to achieve his ends. He is competitive and eager to win and is willing to pay a steep price to win. He is proud of his business accomplishments and at times may appear vain about his financial prowess. He is definitely ambitious for more and can be considered shrewd in some business dealings; however, he does not break the law.

Someone who is a moderate entrepreneur is more honest in his dealings and a bit less manipulative than the high entrepreneur, and he will generally operate within the law.

The low entrepreneur typically manifests no interest in matters of money and frequently finds himself the victim of those less scrupulous than he. He is vulnerable and needs protection in dealings that require astute business judgment.

In general, the entrepreneur may be described as the person who

1. eagerly pursues financial prosperity,
2. is something of a risk taker, especially if he can win big,
3. takes pride in his material possessions,
4. has business acumen and is able to see ways to turn circumstances to his advantage,
5. focuses his energies on the possibilities for the future, not the past,
6. is more of a pragmatist than an idealist,
7. needs to succeed personally,
8. is highly competitive and seeks to win at most activities,
9. is extremely goal-oriented and determined to reach his goals regardless of what may be required, and
10. reads people well and is clever at projecting his best.

ACTIVE

The overachieving individual is disciplined and controlled, sometimes to the point where he strives for perfection. Upon occasion he can expect this same attitude from his associates and subordinates in the organization. His constant search for an ideal state can prove a source of irritation to other people. The entrepreneurial person is highly competitive, risk-prone, and eager to demonstrate his abilities to perform on an individual basis. He will pay lip service to the idea of team effort but basically wants to maintain a separate set of statistics indicating his own successes.

The active individual is almost as different from these two as they are from each other. The active is a friendly, cheerful, and warm person who is genuinely concerned and interested in participating in team activities.

A moderate amount of positive, emotional, responsive sociability, which typifies the active type, is certainly appropriate and useful in many situations. The real warmth and genuine concern that these people demonstrate are oftentimes an uplifting factor at social gatherings or a prime motivator in the work setting. These attributes give the person a certain amount of flash and sparkle at such gatherings, and other people will look to him for both encouragement and entertainment.

The individual with an overabundance of the active trait can cause undue difficulty for others in the organization. Actives genuinely enjoy human companionship almost to the point of not being able to function without it. They delight in being with and around people, thoroughly enjoy the company of others, and in turn want to be liked and appreciated by people. Much like an energetic puppy dog, they are difficult to correct because of their warmth and affection. Overstimulated actives, however, might possess such a desire to be appreciated and approved of by others that their behavior pattern shows certain excesses. They feel they must be loved and will go to great lengths to maintain their relationships in this manner.

Since the active sees everyone as a potential friend and assumes that everyone else feels the same toward him, the active is naturally eager to begin the friendship process. In this process the active can anxiously strive to become buddy-buddy with seemingly everybody, including complete strangers. People with a less emotional disposition can find this good-natured openness an invasion of their privacy and may resent the lack of class displayed by the totally well-meaning active person. Actives develop the reputation for being something of a chatterbox; in truth, they seemingly delight in hearing themselves talk and talk, sometimes apparently for the sake of talking.

Much like the traditional auctioneer, the active apparently appreciates hearing his own voice. He is capable of starting numerous conversations over minute trivia and then proceeding to jabber endlessly about the ramifications of these subjects. If the particularly active person is highly intelligent, others may be absolutely amazed at his wealth of knowledge and breadth of reading. A close inspection of his information, however, will frequently show that he has some knowledge of a variety of topics, but not the breadth that his ability to discuss them might suggest.

The active person demonstrates a high degree of physical energy. He may enjoy watching a sports event on television, as long as he is allowed openly to cheer, boo, and generally carry on during the contest. He is interested in projects as long as they contain some excitement, entertainment, and thrill. The cartoon characters Road Runner and Bugs Bunny in some ways typify this aspect of the active type—boundless energy in search of unending thrills. In the same vein, the active person frequently has many interests. He finds everything and most people interesting and can become easily sidetracked about a given topic. Again, if intelligent, the active can appear to have a breadth of knowledge about a variety of topics, but most active types simply change their temporary emotional focus from one topic to another.

The active person does show a sincere and real interest in other people. The statement "I (almost) never met a person I didn't like" aptly describes many active people. This enthusiasm for helping others can, however, show some negative results. For example, the active may promise the support of his work group to a valuable and worthwhile civic project, only to discover that his peers are not interested in helping. The active can also act somewhat impulsively and form quick alliances. The character D'Artagnan showed such behavior in joining the Three Musketeers and readily pledging himself, "all for one, and one for all."

The fact that the active acts with apparent impulsivity may give him a reputation for being insincere and fickle in his interpersonal dealings. Nothing could be further from the truth. He is entirely well meaning but is sometimes a victim of his overly excitable personality. He would not consciously hurt anyone. The active is a team-oriented individual, and despite his occasionally short-lived enthusiasm for a given task, he can be effective. For example, he is frequently the catalyst to initiate a group project, which can then be completed by other members of the team.

The active is a positive, fun-loving, friendly person who constantly sees a brighter star and is sure that things will improve soon. When he becomes very angry, he loses his temper, but like an erupting volcano the heat passes quickly and the active quickly returns to his optimistic, personable self. Once the outburst passes, he will not hold a grudge, suffers no hard feelings, and is eager to carry on as before. His philosophy is simply that life is too short and human relationships too precious to allow something as silly as an argument to be remembered.

In general, the active may be described as the person who

1. seeks and enjoys the company of other people and is comfortable in social situations,
2. has a positive attitude and is, in general, pleased with the world and enthusiastic about his position in it,
3. has a sunny view of things and has interactions with people that are spontaneous and uninhibited,
4. readily shows his positive feelings, especially his appreciation of human contact,
5. is alertly observant,
6. adapts easily to new things,
7. enjoys laughing and has a warm sense of humor that responds quickly to a good joke,
8. likes being with people, as reflected in his talkative nature,
9. has a high energy level that he enthusiastically spends on doing things, and
10. enjoys the stimulation of having several activities going on at once.

PASSIVE

To review, the overachiever is noted for his self-discipline, personal determination, and belief in the work ethic. The entrepreneur is competitive, driven, and money-motivated to succeed where other more fainthearted souls may fear to tread. The active is socially inclined; he is outgoing, personable, and entirely well meaning, is an eternal optimist, and sees the best in most situations.

The passive trait is in direct contrast to the active. The passive person tends to be cautious, tentative, and slightly unsure. He wants to check and double-check before venturing out too far from home base. In some situations he can be negative and actually feels compelled to point out the dark side of even the most joyous occasion. At times, he is overcome by feelings of self-doubt, is frequently physically tired, and is unsure and ambivalent about his self-worth. He can feel lonely, afraid, and unsure of what forces lurk outside to hurt him. In some ways, he is the person who clings to his blanket and delights in the security of being cared for and protected.

The passive person shares the common baseline of emotionality with the active person, but instead of being exuberant, happy, and optimistic, the passive reverses this orientation and portrays sadness, caution, and a occasional sense of doom. As a financial analyst he sees the return of the depression; as a weather forecaster he tends to see storms on the horizon. He is inclined to believe in people who preach, "Repent; the end is near."

Although it may be difficult for others to appreciate this fact, fear and anxiety haunt the passive. Worse yet, he is unsure of what variables are causing him this anxiety. Like a small child who can sleep only with a bathroom light on, the passive lives in a world composed of Halloween ghosts and goblins ready to cause him instant havoc and ruin at a moment's notice. Despite what other members of the organization might describe as a positive atmosphere, the passive individual sees himself in the eye of a hurricane.

He feels that the current quiet experience is merely the lull before the storm begins. Although noise, change, and commotion alarm him, he can interpret quiet as a sure prelude to a more serious problem. Like the Li'l Abner character Joe Blftzyh, who walks around with a proverbial cloud over his head, the passive person continually foresees unstoppable calamities that may actually possess very real probability of occurring.

The passive may appear tired, listless, and hopelessly fatigued, and he can honestly feel this way. Unfortunately, he can also be like the fifth dwarf, Grumpy, who only Snow White could improve. A comparatively small amount of either physical or mental activity can readily exhaust him. This occurrence may suggest to his working peers that he is lazy or uninterested in the task at hand. This view is simply not true, as the passive person appears simply to have less emotional energy than other people. Sometimes he will stretch himself at work only to come home and then collapse from a long day at the office.

The passive person can be identified by his strong sense of indecisiveness and may accurately be compared to the legendary donkey that, standing between two equidistant bales of hay, starves to death because of his inability to choose between them. In a word, the passive person hates to make decisions of any kind. The decision-making process is a study in frustration for him, as it is an avoidance-avoidance conflict in which he thinks he cannot win. For him, whichever alternative he chooses is bound to have problems and mistakes. Sometimes, deciding not to make a decision is the only possible alternative. In this manner, he hopes that the problems will somehow magically go away and no longer concern him. He will procrastinate and fill his time with relatively unimportant matters that assume temporary magnitude so that he can avoid the implications of the real issues at hand.

The passive individual is quite sensitive and emotional; he is capable of demonstrating a real concern for his fellowman and honestly feels for the mishaps suffered by another. At the same time, he readily responds to warm, positive encouragement from others. Along this line, it is interesting to note that many professional comedians report feeling passive some of the time and that the laughter of their audiences is their prime way of overcoming these feelings. In this way, people such as Jack Benny, Bob Hope, Red Skelton, and Eddie Cantor have reported being able to feel greater self-worth and value. The passive person is constantly checking himself to be sure that he is performing his job duties adequately and performs best when receiving positive reinforcement for his behavior. He is not likely to take credit for his accomplishments, except in extremely safe situations.

It is important to remember that security is very important to the passive individual. Stability is something he constantly strives for, but he never seems to obtain total security in his own eyes. To others his job situation and home life may seem very well grounded and permanent, but the passive will never quite believe it. Because of his interest in security, the passive person is usually interested in a long-term, stable job situation. He will want to keep his job as long as he can, especially if it looks secure and not too demanding of his limited energy.

In a new employment situation, the passive worker may improve more slowly than other workers; however, his improvement will be steady and noticeable. He will endeavor to do the best he can, and to him this means making as few mistakes as possible. His interest in detail reflects this desire to avoid mistakes and is not so much a desire to be concerned with small items.

In general, the passive may be described as the person who

1. is quality control—oriented in his work and personal habits and readily sees the possible mistakes that others will miss,
2. is kind, gentle, and well meaning, although sometimes moody and unsure of his future direction,
3. takes a sometimes slow but generally steady approach,
4. although occasionally cautious, is also a dependable employee whose work will improve at a slow and steady pace,
5. desires security and certainty and does not change jobs frequently,
6. readily empathizes with others' difficulties,
7. is cautious to respond to new ideas and is made uncomfortable by spontaneous or impulsive behavior in others,

8. does not readily show much emotional enthusiasm,

9. sometimes uses his energy worrying, and

10. takes longer time than some to make a decision, as he weighs all possibilities.

SENSITIZED

The last two sections introduced the happy, fun-loving, team-spirited orientation of the active trait and contrasted it with the somewhat dependent, cautious, and frequently unsure attributes of the passive. This section will introduce a person who is shy, introverted, and seclusive but who at the same time is endowed with a rich imagination and is thoroughly capable of enjoying a very varied life by vicariously participating in the activities of others. This person, with the sensitized trait, was characterized in the short story "The Secret Life of Walter Mitty."

This behavior trait comprises only a small part of the adult American population. Children are generally reinforced for aggressive, outgoing, competition-oriented activities that are inconsistent with the development of the sensitized trait. Correspondingly, no behavior trait is more difficult for the majority of the active-prone American culture to understand than the sensitized. Being openly competitive but neighborly and cooperative is simply the American tradition, and people who consider themselves socially outgoing but emotionally responsive sometimes find it difficult to understand or appreciate an individual who can seem happily aloof, somewhat detached, and socially unresponsive.

At first, some other behavior traits feel rebuffed and put down by the apparent inacessibility of the sensitized individual but generally just come to see this person as "nice but somehow different, kind of quiet." The outgoing active seldom stops to realize that perception is a two-way process, as the sensitized individual finds many other behavior traits noisy, inquisitive, and in many ways overbearing. "Just give me some space" might be a frequent comment of the sensitized person to the well-meaning social overtures of the emotionally responsive active individual.

A given degree of the sensitized trait is helpful in an individual behavior pattern. When present to an average degree, the trait provides the individual with a quality of introspection, a sensitivity for the feelings of other people, and an appreciation for the art of social diplomacy. This trait may be compared to a radar screen that is responsible for receiving, interpreting, and understanding the needs, aspirations, and wishes of other people but does not make allowances for action once the incoming information has been received.

The highly sensitized individual is a very perceptive depository for information but finds it difficult to take appropriate actions about it. The moderately sensitized person is correspondingly moderately effective at receiving and acting upon the information. The person with very little of the sensitized traits is poor at receiving information and generally blunders his way through social settings and ignorantly commits faux pas. The person with little of the sensitized trait is sometimes accused of being callous, overly blunt, and lacking in social concern; however, it should be noted that he is generally this way from ignorance rather than deliberate malice.

The most easily observed behavior of the sensitized trait is his reaction to other people in social settings. It is readily apparent that he is shy, quiet, and sometimes uncomfortable. He feels as if he does not belong and would much prefer to absent himself without further ado. Like Casper the Friendly Ghost, the highly sensitized person thoroughly enjoys listening to and watching other people but is frequently uncomfortable when called upon to contribute publicly at a social gathering. In brief, he sees himself as partially living a life according to the Jesuit pattern—"of this world, but not part of it." Sincere attempts on the part of other entirely well-meaning people to enable him to share more fully in group activities can increase his tension and succeed in making him feel even more ill at ease.

The sensitized person is asocial, not antisocial. His sense of quiet reserve and preferred avoidance of social activities stems not in the least from a dislike of people but from his discomfort in the group. His feelings are similar to a glass menagerie: fragile on display and in need of protection. He goes to great lengths to protect himself and accordingly is hard to get to know as well as slow to make new friends. The circle he does make is generally small, and unlike the individual who proclaims having many acquaintances but few friends, the sensitized person has few acquaintances but they are also his close friends. But he sees this situation as a victory of quality over quantity, as his friendships can last for a lifetime and survive occasional upsets or even traumas.

Because the sensitized person projects such a complacent image, it is easy to think that he finds life a dull, humdrum existence, with little excitement and less to look forward to. Such is simply not the case. The sensitized person may lack a traditional action-oriented behavior pattern, but his imagination more than compensates for this lack. He is capable of sitting quietly in an armchair and tracking the last of the Mohicans with Hawkeye, discovering the North Pole with Peary, or scaling Mount Everest with Sir Edmund Hilary. He possesses an endless capacity to entertain himself and thoroughly delights in the activities of his highly creative imagination.

The sensitized person seldom makes the first move toward breaking the ice socially. If someone whom he admires shows an interest in him, however, he will respond warmly and develop a solid relationship with the person. Conversely, he studiously avoids complete strangers and on long-distance rides will bury himself in a book or an equally entertaining session of daydreaming. Again, the sensitized person is not being a snob; he is simply afraid of not being accepted, and rather than risk the loss of self-esteem, he would rather not play the game. For him, it is better to have never loved than to have attempted love and lost.

The sensitized individual displays a behavior pattern typified by seclusion, timidity, and social withdrawal. He delights in being alone and prizes periods of solitude where he is free to indulge his daydreams and creative thinking. He may appear to some to be a typical wallflower (i.e., lacking interest in social activities where there is interaction with other people), but he has a fertile and creative imagination. This rich imagination not only allows him to escape through daydreams to exotic places but can often be used to produce ingenious solutions to long-standing company problems.

The apparently docile and compliant behavior of such an individual may be so extreme that it leads others to assume he can be easily dominated and forced to accept decisions. This assumption, however, is definitely not valid. He is actually quite stubborn, although his resistance may not be expressed overtly. While giving lip service to rules he disagrees with, he will quietly ignore them and will do as he chooses. A person who is moderately sensitized is friendly, and his dealings with people are polite and tactful. The individual who is little sensitized may, conversely, be completely insensitive to the feelings and opinions of others. His most obvious characteristics and patterns of behavior will be determined by the other traits that dominate his personality.

In general, the sensitized may be described as the person who

1. thinks independently and follows his own direction,
2. tends to see criticism and disapproval as personal,
3. is highly tactful and indirect when expressing an opinion,
4. has no difficulty conforming to rules,
5. is extremely creative, with a wealth of ideas,
6. is very comfortable alone,
7. is a perfectionist when it comes to himself and what he sees as personal defects,
8. is frequently a utopian idealist who believes in fairness and equality,
9. has difficulty admitting to himself or others any negative feelings, and
10. can easily grasp intangible and theoretical concepts.

AGGRESSIVE

The previous section provided an introductory chapter to the sensitized behavior trait. This person is shy, introverted, and interpersonally quiet. The source of this introversion is that he is basically socially insecure. He fears social rejection by others and so retreats into his own private world, where he cannot be emotionally hurt or personally embarrassed.

The observable behavior of the aggressive person is just the opposite. He is frequently outspoken, socially domineering, and secretly concerned about others' taking advantage of him. The source of his behavior, however, is also personal insecurity. He is afraid of the outside environment, but rather than withdraw from it, he is "hell-bent for leather" to conquer it.

He almost never admits to the source of his insecurity, but it is at the core of his personality. He tends to live by the philosophy "Strike first and ask questions later." He sees a world filled with people who are jealous of him and his possessions, and he is determined to best others before they take advantage of him. Probably no other behavior trait is more interested in possessing power over other people and receiving the status that comes from holding a high-level position than is the aggressive. He frequently wants to be in charge of whatever activity, group, or organization he is associated with, and he wants everyone to know that he is the leader.

The unique feature about the aggressive individual is that, whatever group he associates with, he feels a burning desire both to try harder and to be "number one." Accordingly, aggressive behavior traits are found in all walks of life, including the corner street gang, bowling leagues, and national politics. In each group, they are constantly striving for a position of visible leadership.

Because the aggressive individual is so competitive about his status and position in the organizational hierarchy, he naturally feels that everyone else has this same orientation. Therefore, he is constantly watching, checking, and monitoring the progress of other people versus that of himself. His thinking follows the dictum "Keep your friends close and your enemies closer," lest they beat him in the competition for advancement. In some ways, the aggressive trait is similar to a big bear that puts its nose in the air, sniffs for food (or power positions), and rumbles off in search of its goal.

He is not devious nor deliberately malicious but may be perceived as anxious and even annoying to some other people whom he sees as competition. Like the grizzly bear that stumbles into a backpacker's camp looking for a little something and coincidentally scares the sleeping hiker half-to-death, the behavior of the motivated aggressive can be disconcerting.

"A woman's place is in the home," "People on welfare are lazy," and "The government is composed of mindless bureaucrats" are typical statements of "truth" that the aggressive trait espouses. This orientation allows the aggressive individual to overcome his own feelings of inferiority and to organize the world into a series of absolutes; that is, most information can be arranged into a "fact" that is either black or white, with little gray area for interpretation.

By judging people, situations, and events in this manner, the aggressive is able to anticipate and orchestrate events that might affect him. As long as he has a stable opinion about something, then he can define himself in terms of that opinion. For example, if all people on welfare are lazy and he is not on welfare, then he thinks he has proof that he is not lazy. The strongly aggressive individual takes this somewhat grandiose and incorrect style of logical deduction and so "proves" his own superiority.

The aggressive may seek out the opinions of a few trusted others, but when he decides upon a given plan of action, he is very slow to change his mind. He does not appreciate being told that his opinion is incorrect or that he is headed in the wrong direction. This attitude can result in all of his subordinates' becoming yes-men. Such an arrangement can provide for harmonious discussions; it may also block the aggressive leader from hearing important outside information.

In a work setting, the aggressive will often seek out a position of leadership. This allows him to acquire the social power and prestige that he feels are so rightfully his. The desire for leadership can, of course, be used to effect a variety of purposes. Billy Graham, for example, has demonstrated a solid leadership of a religious nature, whereas John Brown claimed a religious calling but caused considerable havoc in "Bloody Kansas" prior to the American Civil War. By becoming a leader, the aggressive feels he can effectively implement his ideas and help his associates.

If the aggressive is sufficiently strong in other areas, he may well become successful. Some successful military leaders are representative of the aggressive trait. For example, Julius Caesar, Napoleon, and George Patton appeared to have been this way. Successful trial lawyers, who sometimes have relatively small offices (few partners), like Racehorse Haynes, F. Lee Bailey, and the "King of Torts," Melvin Belli, appear to be examples of this behavior trait.

The aggressive can become an autocrat, an independent ruler whose opinions are always correct. This belief in absolute self-authority is memorialized in the historical voice of the marine drill instructor who barks: "All right, you meatheads, I need three volunteers. You, you, and you just volunteered. Follow the sergeant for your instructions." The more balanced aggressive will also be prepared to accept leadership and responsibility and thoroughly enjoys being in charge. Unlike the high aggressive individual, however, he will not be so dominating in a position of power.

An individual with a moderate or lesser measure of the aggressive trait may be an extremely effective leader, but one with a much different style than the highly aggressive. The moderate aggressive works with people, not over them and neither bulldozes nor argues unnecessarily. The contrast between the high and moderate aggressive may be seen as the difference between leading by intimidation on one hand and by team incentive on the other.

A person with low aggressive tendencies is not usually interested in positions that require substantial managerial talents. His inclination is to evade arguments. He would rather switch than fight, and status is of little importance to him.

In general, the aggressive may be described as the person who

1. enjoys team competition and sees himself as the captain,
2. shows dynamic forcefulness and can be charismatic,
3. may have strong opinions and tends to express them,
4. believes intensely in his own viewpoints,
5. can be overly sensitive to self-perceived slights and reacts harshly to them,
6. enjoys being in charge,
7. sometimes has difficulty seeing others' points of views and can seem overbearing at times,
8. sometimes is hardheaded in his beliefs and may defy authority figures,
9. strongly stands behind his own ideas and methods, and
10. shows a strong sense of determination in the pursuit of his goals.

COMPULSIVE

Thus far the text has described three relatively distinct sets of behavior. The hardworking, self-disciplined, and personally contained orientation of the overachiever was contrasted with the somewhat self-serving, competitive, and money-motivated orientation of the entrepreneur. Then, the common base of the active and passive behavior traits was described in terms of an excess and lack of energy, enthusiasm, and emotional affect. Finally, the sensitized and aggressive behavior traits were defined in terms of sharing common feelings of inferiority but reacting to them in totally different ways. The last behavior trait to be discussed is uniquely different from each of the above and does not have a ready counterpart.

The compulsive behavior trait describes a person noted for his systematic, methodical, and analytical approach to problem solving and his high degree of interest in completing any task assigned to him. Like a precision instrument, the compulsive mechanically, carefully, and meticulously plans and then carries out his day's activities. He strives to accomplish the greatest amount of work in the least amount of time. He is the "old reliable" who faithfully arrives for work on time, diligently performs his responsibilities, and quietly stays later to complete his assignments.

The work habits and orientations of the compulsive individual suggest images of an individual "busy as a little bee," and indeed the task dedication and labor that he demonstrates are in many ways comparable to the organization and structure in animal societies. Books have been written about insect behavior, and ants have been immortalized in the science fiction story "The Army Ants." The compulsive, like the army ants, dislikes interruption in his work and may apparently ignore people's questions or comments addressed to him when engaged in a task.

He is somewhat like the absentminded professor who, when looking through his microscope, fails to hear a caller and continues with his work. It should be remembered that he is not being malicious or deliberately rude to the outside caller; the compulsive is merely engulfed in his work and is honestly unaware of the outsider.

Like the "Little Old Lady Who Lived in a Shoe," the compulsive goes to great lengths to maintain a neat and orderly method to his work. He prides himself on being efficient, but at the same time, appearance per se is not especially important to him. He feels comfortable with an office in a state of "organized chaos" and is uniquely pleased with his own self-styled filing system. Like the great detective Sherlock Holmes, who categorized 141 different types of tobacco but lived in an apparently somewhat disorganized-looking apartment, the compulsive has his own systems and procedures.

The compulsive never enjoys interruptions, but he especially dislikes them when he is mentally "into" his projects. Unfortunately, most offices do not afford him the luxury of a "Do Not Disturb" sign to hang on his door. His disappointment and dislike at being disturbed during these times will pass quickly, and he will soon settle into his work and become his normally preoccupied self. It has been said that the only time anyone saw Kant, the German philosopher, become disturbed was when he was interrupted taking his carefully planned walks.

The compulsive is known for being an exceptionally thorough person in planning his actions. In this way, he may be compared to a master chess or bridge player who constantly analyzes his positions with one eye and antici-pates long-range strategy with the other. Individuals with these skills are frequently credited with being military planners, and many military acade-my graduates possess this ability. General Douglas MacArthur was known for making large-scale and exacting plans for a major military maneuver and then, after the plan had been effected, asking about the progress of a certain five-man squad in an exact area. (Of course, he also possessed a pho-tographic memory.)

The compulsive is sometimes thought of as being a nitpicker perfectionist who obviously loves details; this description is not necessarily the case. The compulsive is not so much enamored with details per se as merely focused on them to the exclusion of the rest of the project. He sometimes cannot see the forest for the trees; he is not concerned about winning the war or even the battle, but he is concerned that his uniform exactly complies with regula-tions. In work situations where attention to detail is important, the com-pulsive serves a very useful function.

Due to the compulsive's exhaustive consideration of detail, he tends to form firm opinions that are carefully considered and logically constructed. Like a lawyer carefully compiling evidence for a court case, the compulsive individual thrives on the use of deductive logic and taking carefully mea-sured steps to reach his conclusions. He is not necessarily close-minded as the aggressive trait can be, however, as he will change his mind when presented with a new series of facts. In brief, his mind operates like a machine that analyzes information and simply reports conclusions. In some ways, the compulsive person can be compared to the character Mr. Spock in the *Star Trek* movies.

The compulsive behavior trait shows a high need for achievement, and he receives a good deal of satisfaction from accomplishing his tasks on time. The more work responsibility he accepts and completes, the better he feels. For him, it is important that the work be completed. It is not critical that he receive the credit for it. With all his concern for using time well in accomplishing something worthwhile to him, (whether others think it is important or not), he does not consider himself necessarily more important than anyone else. The compulsive generally feels that everyone is important, each in his own way.

It is easiest to comprehend the compulsive behavior trait by focusing on his appetite for working on projects and assignments methodically and with a preoccupation with details. He finds pleasure in making plans, arranging his ideas in logical sequences, and assuming the responsibility for assignments, which he then completes by working methodically and meticulously. He prefers to concentrate on one assignment at a time and carry it systematically, step by step, to completion.

Individuals with a high degree of the compulsive trait are uncommon in our society. Most people usually have an average amount of this trait, which is, in general, adequate for most administrative positions. They share the same general traits as the highly compulsive, but not to such an extreme degree.

On the other hand, these traits are almost lacking in the low compulsive person, who typically has no liking for detailed work and has no idea how to organize his work. He routinely delegates administrative chores while he consumes much time redoing work or trying to define a system from which to work. This low compulsive behavior can, however, be balanced if an overachiever trait is present. In this situation, an individual can compensate by approaching a task with the attitude "I dislike doing the details, but I can make myself do them because I want to complete the job."

In general, the compulsive may be described as the person who

1. plays the role of good ally in the planning stage of a project,
2. readily shows a sense of thorough workmanship,
3. prefers getting the job done himself rather than delegating it,
4. does well with the details of a job and likes to have the sole responsibility for an assignment,
5. is deliberate, logical, and businesslike in his approach,
6. speaks of work-related matters in a very detailed way,

7. takes pride in completing a task,

8. is very directed in his approach and dislikes being interrupted or sidetracked from his goal,

9. can be depended upon to have as his priority keeping a job on schedule and according to plan, and

10. prefers task involvement to social interaction.

BEHAVIOR STYLE

Although the seven traits were defined and measured separately, they actually combine and interact to define a person's everyday behavior or behavior style. A person's behavior style is a way of classifying the manner in which he customarily behaves and in which he interacts with his social environment. Moreover, a single trait is not sufficient to define real people. When these traits combine in a person, a more realistic description is possible. Let's review the idea of a person's behavior style by analyzing how the overachiever and entrepreneur traits combine to form the overachiever-entrepreneur behavior style.

The overachiever behavior trait represents a unique individual who can be identified and analyzed as such. At the same time, the overachiever trait is unique in that it interacts with and influences each of the other traits. A person whose behavior is dominated by the overachiever will appear as a unique person, but most people possess a reasonable but not overwhelming amount of this trait. For these people the overachiever trait will act as a control function with the other traits. This combination of overachiever and each of the other traits will be useful in describing most behavior styles. It is not sufficient, for example, to say that a person is high on the entrepreneur trait; it is also necessary to indicate how much of the overachiever trait he possesses as well.

Why? Because, for example, the person who is high on both the overachiever and entrepreneur traits is a much different person from the one who is low on the overachiever and high on the entrepreneur. We would call the former person controlled and might describe him as showing a fully functional temperament. The latter person might be described as a prisoner of his own desires. He might show little respect for the rights and feelings of others and generally be interested in satisfying his personal, social, and physical needs without due consideration for the rights of others.

The individual with a high amount of the entrepreneur and with a high degree of the overachiever trait, the overachiever-entrepreneur, is both self-disciplined and money-motivated. He seeks a position of higher status and focuses his energies on acquiring additional material possessions, but he does so with a good deal of self-discipline and emotional control. In some ways, he can be compared to the fictional British Secret Service agent James

Bond. He is smooth, slick, and socially polished. He apparently enjoys the good life, but he also lives according to an internally regulated set of rules that ensures that he follows a generally professional mode of conduct. He may want to satisfy his desires quickly, but he will generally forestall his immediate impulses and suppress his first response. He likes the idea of delayed gratification and is willing to forgo the immediate pleasure of most enjoyments for a possible greater pleasure to be had after completing a task.

The person with a solid degree of the overachiever and average amount of the entrepreneur will generally show a modest interest in being competitive, driven, and eager for business success. He may consider himself as money-motivated as most people, but he is not driven by a desire for more things. He probably prides himself on having a balanced life-style. He enjoys his professional life and his personal life, and he sees himself as progressing in an orderly manner to achieve a reasonable and satisfying life. He is not unduly clever, but neither is he readily suckered or sold something he does not want. He is aware of unethical and shady business practices, but he does not subscribe to them, nor is he susceptible to them.

The person with a solid degree of the overachiever and a low amount of the entrepreneur needs to be protected in some ways from the practicalities of real business life. This person can be considered naive and almost simplistic and unassuming to the point of believing even the most strained tales of salesmanship. These people are too unassuming, and to some degree they can be taken advantage of by others less scrupulous than themselves. They are completely honest and aboveboard to the point of being homespun. They possess an endearing quality of truth, honesty, and loyalty that can border on the saintly, but they need to become more hardened and experienced in life to be more effective in the real world.

This same form of description can be applied to other combinations of the behavior traits discussed in this chapter.

3

Interpreting the 120 Questionnaire

This chapter contains examples of responses to the 120 Questionnaire. Typically the completed 120 Questionnaire is the first piece of hard information that the interviewer has about the candidate and that is completed in the candidate's own handwriting and expresses his own thoughts and opinions. Properly used, it can be very revealing about the candidate.

A careful analysis of the completed 120 Questionnaire will help the interviewer form impressions of the candidate's interpersonal skills and behavior style. These impressions are possible because responses from different behavior styles are included for each question. (You will notice that examples of each of the seven traits are not included for every question. The most frequently excluded examples are for the compulsive trait, since research indicates that it is the least common trait in the general population.) The interviewer can compare the candidate's responses to a given question with the responses of people representing the different behavior styles. For example, the entrepreneur is typically interested in money, short-term advancement, and individual rewards. These interests will be reflected in his answers to the 120 Questionnaire.

Reviewing the 120 Questionnaire should enable the interviewer to understand better the candidate's interpersonal skills and behavior style. Naturally, these initial impressions need to be checked with additional information, but a review of the completed 120 Questionnaire begins the learning process.

This chapter is a review and explanation of the completed 120 Questionnaire. It contains a sequential and detailed review of the candidate's written responses to questions about his education, work history, preferred bosses and working conditions, future goals, and a series of other work-related topics. It concludes with a series of sentence completion statements that allow the candidate to project himself further onto the page.

Appendix A contains a blank 120 Questionnaire. Selected question topics covered in the 120 Questionnaire follow.

NAME

Clearly, this entry by itself will not typically reveal a significant amount of information about the candidate; however, it is worthwhile to consider every piece of information on the questionnaire because each piece of information can be combined with data from other entries to tell us something significant about a candidate. With that thought in mind, let's review the person's name. Our name is our first indication of identity. A person with an ordinary name will react quite differently from a person with a very dignified name or a person with a somewhat silly name. Some think of their names as an adornment while others think very little of their names. If a person insists on the use of a title or Jr. or III, it may indicate something of his personality, economic class, or upbringing. If the individual has substituted an initial for his first name or first and middle names, he may be somewhat defensive or he may be a comfortable, casual individual who is sharing his nickname with you.

ADDRESS

Again, the person's address is not going to provide you with a significant, decision-making piece of information, but knowing the area from which the candidate comes could be very enlightening. For example, the state in which the person resides may give some clue to his mind-set. The individual from San Diego, California, (who may have an interest in surfing) probably has an attitude altogether different from the individual from Queens (who may be a devoted New York Mets fan), as well as different life experiences. Living in the city implies a different set of values from those of the country dweller.

INFLUENCES TO DEVELOPMENT

Describe your development. What factors (family, education, work, etc.) influenced you to be the person that you are today?

Pay attention to whether or not the individual takes a positive or negative view toward himself today. Does he blame others for what he has become? Does all of the credit go to him? Does he hold onto childhood influences as being most important and influential, or is his view broader, more mature?

EDUCATION

Name and location of school, major and minor courses, dates attended, diploma or degree, and average grade.

An individual's education gives the first indications of his potential for achievement. It also shows how early in life this need for achievement, or lack thereof, begins. It is not an accurate indicator of continued success in the job environment. If an individual actually lists a grade point average by its numeric value (e.g., 3.5), this says something about the precision of his thinking. Remember that people often remember their grade point average as being a bit higher than it was.

Pay particular attention to specialty courses of study, where the candidate has tried to solve a problem, or, better, what he sees as a weakness in himself through schooling (e.g., public speaking courses, career planning, therapy for a speech defect). When there are a number of higher education institutions mentioned, it can be assumed that the individual had trouble deciding on his vocation or that he was unable to settle on a school in which he was comfortable and satisfied. This information can be an indication of a lack of direction or clear-cut career planning; look at it in the context of the other information. Remember also to consider the applicant's intelligence in the context of the interview.

Grades and schooling have long been discredited as accurate indicators of real intelligence. Do an informal evaluation of the individual's intellectual level yourself. Consider his use of vocabulary, his variety of sentence structure, and his clarity of expression. Also, remember that more intelligent people will generally answer questions more quickly, particularly the open-ended questions. In general, does he use his grammar skills and vocabulary to make his point or to impress the interviewer with his business jargon? There are points that can be made about the individual's personality from this section, but only in light of the other information offered. The name of the school that the candidate attended may tell you something about him and his need for a feeling of prestige, sports accomplishment, academic excellence, or social life.

Assumptions are made about intelligence, for example, that the majority of people fall in the area of average intelligence, with others in the low or high ranges. The behavior style of an individual is directly affected by his intelligence. People will use powers of reasoning to enhance their personalities and goals or may constantly seek to compensate for a seeming or actual lack of reasoning skills. We will discuss some examples of the high intelligent behavior types and allow the reader to draw his inferences from these.

The entrepreneur is constantly scheming to get ahead in career and financial gain; therefore, when this set of values is backed by high intelligence, the individual becomes a highly clever, money-motivated, and competitive individual in the business sense. He is unscrupulous and unpredictable. As intelligence drops in the entrepreneur type, so does his influence. The entrepreneur who possesses average to low intelligence will have mainly short-term goals and a more simplistic approach, as he is seeking immediate gratification for his efforts.

The highly intelligent active will be a very popular, fun-loving individual with quick, insightful humor. He will be unbeatable in banter and social repartee and play the crowd with intelligent wit. As intelligence drops, the active looks for group enthusiasm and high-energy types of entertainment rather than relying on his wit to attain approval.

The passive type will use his cleverness to make his negative outlook known. He can be caustic in his remarks once he is hired and may often appear overly cold. This behavior is his approach to attaining the approval and reassurance that he needs from his superiors and that he is unlikely to get. During emotional times the passive becomes actually more warm and compassionate; the highly intelligent passive almost makes up for his previous attitude this way, but the less intelligent levels lack the perception either to be so biting or to make up for this attitude.

UNFINISHED LEVELS OF EDUCATION

Did you interrupt or fail to finish any level of your education? If so, please explain.

The reasons given for the interruption of studies or for leaving school altogether may hide some other, more accurate reason. They may also indicate how highly the person values his education. He may place the blame anywhere but on himself or may just give an inaccurate description of the events ending in his leaving. Again, it is important to gather information from the other questions to analyze responses accurately.

Each behavior type's different set of values and motivations will show up here. The overachiever may quit school to earn money but will most likely finish his education. The entrepreneur will take the next risk that comes along, such as an opportunity to travel or a business venture. The active will get bored quickly and show an emphasis on social activities, fraternities, and so on that may cause grades to suffer. Passive types get discouraged easily, enroll off and on, complete their degrees in night school, and grasp at anything that might make them more valuable in the workplace. The sensitized individual longs for individualized attention; he will be unhappy in a large institution. The aggressive will leave to do something else that seems more or equally challenging and then return to finish his education early. The compulsive type will just begin something else, but he will be sure of the dates of the beginning and ending of his education.

Overachiever

"I dropped out to support my mother and younger brothers and sister when my father died. Worked full-time in oil fields for one year, made money, and returned to school full-time."

Entrepreneur

"Had a chance to travel so I took it; I wasn't doing well or getting much out of it anyway, so I dropped out."

Active

"I got involved with fraternity partying too much, didn't study enough, and flunked out."

Passive

"I'm working toward my degree at night and take one class a semester when I can." Night school might suggest an overachiever but often is an indication of the passive's grasp for security, especially if he takes courses intermittently at a mediocre school when he easily has access to a better one. His primary motivation may be his belief that he will make his job more secure if he has a degree.

Sensitized

"I felt the school was too big and impersonal; I was just a number. The professors were unapproachable, and the whole process too mechanical."

Aggressive

"I wasn't doing well, so I dropped out and signed up with the army. I got myself straightened out, went back, and got my degree in 2½ years."

Compulsive

You will find in his answer the exact month and year he left school to begin something else.

FAVORITE COURSES

What were your favorite courses in school? Why did they appeal to you?

Subjects favored in school are often aligned with skill levels. People with more analytical skills will do better in math and science and will favor these subjects because they have done well in them. They indicate areas of interest or special ability. Look for a common thread between the courses, as people rarely are interested in every subject equally.

People tend to prefer courses in which they do fairly well. If someone, for example, likes English literature better than calculus, he probably has more competence with words than with numbers and vice versa. The subjects listed can provide clues. For instance, they might indicate a preference for analytical thinking or ability or interest in a specific area. The applicant's explanation of his interests in a historical context can supply clues to his background and personality. Was he really fascinated by these subjects, and is he discriminating in his choices? Rarely are people interested in everything; most need to focus their interests to do well. The subjects chosen may reveal something about an applicant's behavior type. For example, accounting requires a close attention to detail, and those who choose it are that way. People who themselves are somewhat insecure or who are interested in social service may find psychology appealing.

Compulsive types will choose a subject that allows them to pay close attention to detail and figures, while English may attract the sensitized types, encourage them to expand their imaginations, and allow them a lot of reading and analysis time. The reason given for the favorite subject may tell a lot more than the choice itself. The overachiever may enjoy getting a correct, definite answer, while the sensitized would like to ponder different "answers" in philosophy or literature. The aggressive type might lean toward politics or history for role models and to learn leadership tactics from the past. The passive will favor practical subjects that he thinks will give him an edge in life. The active type will favor something that he thought was exciting or would lead to something exciting and that actually kept his attention.

The choice of favorite subjects may reflect the intelligence level of an applicant, although the reason a subject is chosen often reveals more than does the specific subject chosen.

Overachiever

"Math, chemistry, physics, and debate. They're all based on logic, so there's either a right or a wrong answer, and if you're wrong, you know you can get the right answer if you just think logically."

Entrepreneur

"Business administration. I've always liked to explore the workings of the stock market and the world of finance. I see the study of business as preparation for the real world. I especially like real estate and aim for a sales career."

Active

"Aeronautical engineering. Commercial piloting really used to excite me."

Passive

"Money and banking because it prepared me for my career. Also, the material was presented at a pace that was slow and regular so you didn't feel overloaded with information or work."

Sensitized

"English literature. My imagination was really excited by the imagery of Keats and Shelley. Music and art appealed to me because they required originality, creative and imaginative thinking."

Aggressive

"History. The subject bored me, but the teacher was a real leader who made it interesting. I admired that."

TROUBLESOME COURSES

What courses gave you the most trouble? Why do you think you had problems with them?

These courses will indicate subjects in which the candidate did poorly or that he values negatively. His reasoning may show a general reaction when faced with difficulty and its resulting anxiety. Look for rationalization or admission that the subject was truly difficult. Does he blame his own failings or the unprepared professor? He may simply dislike courses that he found difficult to grasp. The overachiever would rebel against the idea of plugging data into a formula and the memorization required in different types of chemistry. The active would also do poorly with memorization, while the compulsive may dislike any subject based on concepts and not the concrete. The sensitized may dislike any type of performance class where he would feel inspected and embarrassed.

Overachiever

"Inorganic chemistry. There were too many formulas to understand and memorize, and I just couldn't do it."

Entrepreneur

"Latin. It's a dead language you can't use with anyone; it's of no practical use and a waste of time to study. Biology. The teacher wasn't at all good." (Projection of responsibility for failure onto the teacher and denial of personal responsibility can be seen here.)

Active

"World history, because of the endless memorization of boring dates."

Passive

"World history. There were many 'pop' quizzes, and they were hard to prepare for."

Sensitized

"Speech. Six speeches were required, and giving them was extremely embarrassing for me."

Aggressive

"Geography. It just didn't interest me."

COURSES IN FUTURE

What other courses or supplementary instruction would you like to pursue?

The type of list offered here will say quite a bit about the candidate. Is he looking to improve an area in which he feels he is weak or needs some work? Some candidates will list many types of courses without having shown any tendency toward them in the past. Perhaps he means to pursue all of these but just does not have the necessary inclination or drive. If he is aware of the position for which he is applying, he may list a course that would help him in that position and that would show his conscientious research of the position or his awareness and use of the employer's expectations. A list of areas that need improvement either will show an individual's self-awareness and insight or may be a warning to the employer not to expect too much in this area.

An applicant could easily answer with almost anything, as he knows he will not be made actually to follow through. A long list given by someone who has done little in the past may indicate good intentions with little drive behind them, except, perhaps, guilt. The courses may indicate where an applicant's current interests lie. A person who is interested in a Dale Carnegie course differs from one planning to learn a technical field.

Are the courses related to the job he is applying for or to his present occupation? The list may reveal his perception of what is expected, even if he does not actually intend to follow through. It may also reveal his insight or his deficiencies. A person, for example, applying for a job as a secretary whose list includes a refresher course in shorthand may be feeling insecure about this skill and suggesting you should not demand too much.

The overachiever will pursue something he has already begun or take a self-improvement course. The entrepreneur will give the interviewer what he thinks the interviewer wants to hear. This list will be quite unreasonable and incredible, such as a side career or another advanced degree. The active will mention something that is unrelated to career or education but that is social, like acting, wine tasting, or cooking, and that is entertaining and adds to social graces. The passive type will pursue his security. His goals will be similar to those of the overachiever in reality but will be less impressive and geared more toward his goal of job and general security. The sensitized will show an appreciation for the arts or a special interest in an area of study in a period of literature or history.

Again, you must assess this question in context and in combination with the responses to other questions.

Overachiever

He will most likely choose courses that will continue his training in a given field (e.g., "The Dale Carnegie course to improve my public speaking; parts 2 and 4 of the C.L.U. [Certified Life Underwriter], since I've already completed the others") although he may wish to take courses in a diversity of areas simply for self-improvement.

Entrepreneur

He may express goals that he thinks will influence you favorably but that may be impractical, such as: "I may possibly get a law degree because the world is becoming more and more complex" (even though he has made no effort toward starting such a degree) or "I'll get a real estate license and sell part-time."

Active

This applicant might suggest a subject that is completely unrelated to his career but that hints at an enjoyment of social activities: "There's a wine-tasting class that appeals to both my wife and me. It's a chance for us to enjoy something together."

Passive

As with other responses, this response of the passive individual will reflect a preoccupation with security: "Continue working toward my M.A. and possibly get a Ph.D. someday." The goals may be as unrealistic as those of the entrepreneur, but the underlying motivation will be security. Additionally, the goals, for example, law and real estate as opposed to business administration, will not be as directly aimed toward gaining status or making money.

Sensitized

The courses suggested by this individual will often reveal an artistic bent, such as literature, art, or music, or he may wish to pursue a personal interest: "American history before 1900 really intrigues me, and I'd like to study it further."

SIGNIFICANT TEACHERS

Which of your teachers had the most effect on you? Tell us why you remember him or her so well.

Watch how the candidate describes this individual. This person represents an early authority figure in the candidate's life, and he must claim him as an either positive or negative influence. For the most part, the candidate will list attributes to which he aspires himself and will usually give a positive description. Choosing a teacher from early childhood may show something of the individual's clinging to the past or his dependence on parent figures. Note the way the candidate describes the individual and when his influence became prominent in the candidate's life. For what values does he show a positive regard in his description? Are the qualities he mentions ones that he already possesses or sees himself as possessing?

Evaluate his enthusiasm for the teacher and the positive effects derived from the experience. Exactly how does he describe the teacher and the benefits received? How warmly does he describe the relationship? What methods of control were used by this teacher? Was he or she mainly interested in fostering freedom of expression or in maintaining strict authoritarian control? To what extent are there identification by the applicant with the teacher and a sharing of perceived attributes?

Overachievers will mention a high school teacher who was difficult but fair in his dealings with people and who had high expectations for himself and his students. The entrepreneur will admire someone who he thinks would be successful in business, who had attributes like social graces, natty dress, and smooth manner, and who encouraged independence and achievement. The active will be very warm in his description of a favorite authority figure. The passive type will show his dependent nature by recalling a grade school teacher whom he will describe in warm terms but who was a definite authority figure. The sensitized will describe a college professor who inspired him to think, whose comments were "insightful" and "interesting."

The aggressive type will admire strength and a teacher or coach who pushed for results.

Overachiever

The overachieving personality characteristically recollects a high school or college teacher who was demanding and perfectionistic in his expectations for himself and his students and whom the overachiever describes as being fair.

Entrepreneur

This personality type will regard highly a teacher who handled himself smoothly and encouraged independence.

Active

This person speaks warmly of influential authority figures and views them very positively.

Passive

The passive personality type will usually remember and describe a grade school teacher and suggest emotional dependence. He will give a warm, feeling portrayal of the person, but in authoritarian terms.

Sensitized

This individual is likely to choose an exceptionally learned college professor whose comments were insightful and who planned his class well and made the subject interesting.

Aggressive

An athletic coach, whom he describes as warm and friendly but demanding and strong, is frequently remembered by this candidate.

EXTRACURRICULAR ACTIVITIES

Which extracurricular activities were you involved in while in school or college? List clubs, organizations, sports, academic events, music, offices, etc.

This area is useful in indicating many things. The number and variety of activities the candidate lists here will show how he directs his energy, how widespread his interests are, and how he seeks to better himself. He had to choose these particular activities from a probably large variety. Do they imply a wish to improve himself or a hidden skill that has been developed (e.g., debating or organizational skills involved in some types of charity work)? These may most directly parallel personality and provide the most insight.

What kinds of activities did the applicant enjoy in school? Understanding both what he has and what he has not done can be useful in discerning patterns of interest and values. Did he engage in a few or many activities?

How wide a range did these cover? Which were of most value to him, and in which did he participate the most? The answers to these questions reveal how discriminating he is, how able to commit himself, and how motivated. Did some activities involve other people, or were they solitary? Did some entail competition or require cooperation? Did he hold a leadership position? Is anything intrinsically implied by the activities? For instance, to be successful, a debater must cultivate his ability to express himself.

The overachiever will list somewhat competitive, intellectual activities and leadership in many of them. Entrepreneurs will have whatever positions of authority are available (e.g., pledge trainer), organizational activities, business pursuits, and intramural athletics. The active individual will continue to follow the pattern of social activities. He will be homecoming king, orientation leader for his college, or a band leader or pep squad leader. The passive may avoid school activities altogether, as he most likely did not find his upper-level education to be adequate or enjoyable because of the pressures he put on himself. The sensitized individual will list intellectual pursuits or no activities at all. The aggressive will be a leader where he can and value competitive activities. The compulsive will seek detail-oriented positions like class treasurer or finance committee.

The choice of activities is a reflection of personality structure and can increase insight in analyzing behavior.

Overachiever

"Debate team, chess club, the Knights (a service club), president of the Young Republicans."

Entrepreneur

"Business fraternity; pledge trainer and president of my fraternity; active in intramural athletics—we were volleyball champs during my sophomore year."

Active

"Guided visiting high school seniors around the campus; drill team; social chairman for homecoming; member of the pep squad."

Passive

"None."

Sensitized

"None" or "Astronomy club, chess club, and honor society."

Aggressive

"Debate team—I like the challenge of a good argument; intramural athletics—I was quarterback, and we won the football championship for our fraternity."

Compulsive

"Secretary of the finance committee and sophomore class treasurer."

AWARDS AND HONORS

What honors, prizes, distinctions, etc. have you earned?

Pay attention to these awards. Are they for actual participation or for simple attendance? Do they show a bent toward leadership? The items listed here reveal those areas or activities in which the applicant was probably most interested and committed. Note what these imply about emotional and social maturity, intellectual interest, and so on.

Overachiever

"I received a state scholarship to pay for ½ of my tuition; my high school senior class voted me most likely to succeed; came in third in the state debating championship."

Entrepreneur

"Captain of the football team and president of my business fraternity in my senior year."

Active

"Voted most popular in my junior year."

Sensitized

"Vice president of the chess club; placed second in the state science fair in my junior year."

FINANCING EDUCATION

How did you pay for your education (family, scholarship or grant, loan, G.I. Bill, job earnings, etc.)? Please give particulars.

Was his education completely paid for, or did he help with the financing? A high degree of commitment is manifested by someone who works his way through college. On the other hand, paying partially for his education may indicate the person dislikes being dependent on his parents.

The fact that parents pay for college education is not necessarily an indication of the personality of the student. An overachiever may simply accept this help as a circumstance and dedicate himself to studying and self-improvement. The entrepreneur will also accept the support but spend minimum time studying and the rest in play. When any student does work, the kind of work chosen might be an indication of behavior type but is more likely a factor of physical size, intelligence, and lucky opportunity.

Entrepreneur

"I did some bartending and was a waiter at the 901 Club—the hours were flexible and the pay good."

Active

"Sold Christmas trees during the winter and pots and pans in the summer. It was a great way to meet people, and I got some experience selling."

Passive

"I was a clerk in the admissions office—the pay was low, but the people were nice."

Aggressive

"I paid half by working summers in construction, and half was paid by my parents."

MOST PREFERRED POSITION

Which of your jobs or posts did you enjoy the most? Why?

We cannot give any guidelines as to what job an applicant should prefer. In most cases, he will have no difficulty choosing a favorite job. If he does, you might question his ability to discriminate or involve himself. Many will prefer their present job. This response is to be expected, especially if they have made gains in responsibility and authority. If the person does favor the present job, you will be led as a matter of course to question why he wants to change. If he chooses an earlier job, this response may be a clue that he is continually discontented or cannot handle added responsibility appropriately. What does he particularly like about the job chosen, and is this a reflection of his personality?

A salesman who says he does not like sitting behind a desk reveals his restlessness and dissatisfaction with sedentary tasks. What type of job is chosen, and what does this imply about the applicant? A declaration that he enjoys being a waiter because of the responsibility involved implies something about his concept of responsibility. Does the applicant incline toward public accounting or human resources?

As in other areas, each personality type will project his own values onto the jobs he had.

Overachiever

"I enjoyed all my jobs; each was, at the time, a good fit for me and what I needed for my advancement. I'm looking forward to greater future challenges but don't regret my past decisions at all."

Entrepreneur

Because he exists in the immediate present, his attention usually centers on his present job, and he gives suitable responses such as "Commission salesman; it's a perfect combination—the harder I work, the more I earn."

Active

"Personnel administrator. There was a lot of variety and change in the work. I liked that aspect, and I love meeting and helping people."

Passive

"Quality control engineer. The income was steady, there were clear guidelines to
  follow, and I was not overloaded with duties."

JOB HISTORY

*Name of employer, where employed, nature of business, position descrip-
tion, immediate supervisor, dates of employment, starting and ending income (salary/commission), reason for leaving.*

This question is one of the most significant elements of this evaluation.
This history, though it may include some distortion of facts, shows the
applicant's opportunities, choices, interests, obstacles, growth, failures, and
responsibilities as an adult. Notice his progress or lack of it. Did he frequently change his location or direction? Did he find it impossible to remain
at one activity or company? Was there an increase in his salary and responsibilities?

What kinds of things did he fail to include? These could be signs of poor
job performance or an inability to get along with his employer. If he presents
many rationalizing explanations, such as "It was the end of the job" or
"There was no work," they may be a clue. Can you see any pattern or cycle
in his work history? Are there any indications of dissension or personality
conflicts? Although the stated reason for leaving may be true, you cannot
always assume it is true. This record is evidence of his efforts, and though
luck may have been some factor in the level of achievement reached, whether
it was high or low does reflect his personality. If, despite all his efforts, he has
never gone beyond stock clerk but believes he could be company president,
something is obviously awry.

There is some tendency for certain behavior types to gravitate toward
certain industries. Frequently, the entrepreneur will be in sales, especially
commission sales or areas that require little training. Passive individuals are
attracted to government civil service, where salaries are sometimes low but
security is generally high. Sensitized types are generally selected by institutions of higher learning, which emphasize research and creative thinking.
Highly aggressive or passive individuals can be equally attracted to the
military. Almost by definition, accounting appeals to persons who possess a
greater than average measure of compulsiveness. Rapid advancement in
managerial levels is usually accomplished by people with a good amount of
the overachiever or aggressive in their personalities.

An individual's career decisions tell much about him, and what he has
experienced over a period of time will have affected his personality. The
person who has sold the *Encyclopaedia Britannica* for five years will have a
different set of experiences from one who has tended bar, and each will be
affected and altered differently by the path he chose. Therefore, it is wise to
pay attention to the effects of various job environments on the personality.

Do not expect a 20-year-civil servant to become a dynamo in a vital sales organization. Correspondingly, someone who has held five sales positions with different companies in three years is unlikely to become an employee with long-term loyalty unless it fits his needs and desires of the moment.

LEAST FAVORITE JOB

Which of your jobs or posts did you enjoy least? Why?

In this question the candidate must consider some part of his experience negatively. Three interpretations of a blank response can be considered: he may be very accepting of change and adapts well to new places and activities; he may not be very discriminating about his experiences; or he may be wary of the effect his response will have on the evaluator. Many people are not averse to telling about a least favorite job, and one can tell many things about likes, dislikes, and personality from this response. Some people show their insecurity by rejecting a job because they think they do not have the skills needed to be successful. Others may feel their first job had too little responsibility or freedom, while they feel their last job had the responsibility for the whole department. Look for a specific reason a candidate rejected this job rather than another. Some will simply hate failing.

The compulsive type will be critical of sloppy figure work or record keeping. The aggressive type will dislike a job in which he was immediately criticized for being disruptive. The sensitized will devalue a job that embarrassed him or caused him to fail.

In general, the same concerns as previously stated apply here; that is, people tend to project their own attitudes onto situations.

Sensitized

"I sold cookware door-to-door one summer while I was in college. I failed miserably; I wasn't comfortable calling on strangers."

Aggressive

"I took a government job when I left school and got in trouble for speaking my mind and giving suggestions for improvement. I simply understood things better and knew more than the people there."

Compulsive

"The Corleone Olive Oil Import Company. I worked in their credit department and couldn't stand their lack of organization. They kept no records."

COMPANY ATTITUDE

Select any company or firm for which you have worked and relate its feeling and position toward people.

This response can be expressed either positively or negatively, although a candidate is more likely to opt for a positive approach. The level of his objectivity, insight, and sophistication can be measured in this response. Does he describe the company as helpful, generous, or fair in its treatment of employees? Does he refer to its status within the industry or the security it affords? What specifically does the applicant value in an organization and its policies, for example, close personal bonds or fringe benefits?

Entrepreneur

"The ABC Company. They gave the sales agents free rein with dependable backup. But then there was a change in management, and they made you check in every day. So I left, and soon after most of the good regional people did, too."

Active

"The last place I worked. Their attitude toward their employees was very affirming. They believed that their employees were their most important asset."

Passive

"Old Reliable Widget was a really stable organization that had terrific benefits. They took care of their employees, unlike the company where I now work, which provides no security at all."

Sensitized

"Amalgamated Can. The only connection I really had to the company was through my boss, and he was impossible to please—a real know-it-all, who'd chew you out in front of everyone."

SCHOOL-AGE EMPLOYMENT

What part-time, temporary or off-season jobs, not included below, did you have as a youth?

From this question we can make some assumptions about the candidate's early sense of responsibility and industriousness. Men will often recall jobs cutting lawns, shoveling snow, and managing newspaper routes. Years ago this response was less true of women, but, increasingly, women will report early job responsibilities as well. Having a job at a very early age may indicate an overachiever or entrepreneur behavior developing.

FUTURE JOB AND SALARY

What kind of work would you enjoy doing 5 years from now? How much would you want to earn then?

This response will provide another clue about the candidate's view of himself and his behavior. Look at how he sees himself. Are his goals realistic or unrealistic? Are his plans in line with where he has been and where he is heading in his life? Does he mention his family? The applicant will present here his vocational goals and objectives for the next five years. Notice the way in which he projects himself into the future. Are his projections modest and cautious or impractical? Do his goals correspond to the possibilities offered by the job for which he is applying?

The overachiever will have high goals, with a large salary increase. The entrepreneur will be unrealistic in his projection, especially in the area of future earnings. The active will mention the next level as he perceives it, and the passive will consider what he is earning now, with inflation figured in and security for his wife and children. He may actually give a percentage increase over what he is making now. The sensitized may not make a material prediction. He is interested in maintaining what he has now, rather than gaining more. The aggressive type will predict a large amount of responsibility and an accompanying salary reflecting his accomplishments.

Small but significant clues to an applicant's personality type can be found in the answer to this question.

Overachiever

"I usually feel that work is its own reward, but I'd like to own the shop that I now manage and have a salary and override of $75–125,000."

Entrepreneur

The entrepreneur may name an unrealistic figure when predicting his future earnings. This rule of thumb is less reliable in the young, but if such unrealistic figures are presented by someone over 25, it is highly likely you are dealing with an entrepreneurial type.

Active

"I want to be employed in management of some sort."

Passive

Remember, his chief concern is security, as reflected by a statement such as: "The way money is today, I'd need at least a 7 percent increase each year. Of course, with inflation increasing, this might be an underestimate."

Sensitized

"Money isn't my main objective. I'd just like enough to keep up my present way of living."

Aggressive

"I want to be in sales management, so I can put together my own unit. In five years I see myself as divisional manager over all of the western states, with income commensurate with such a position."

FAVORITE SUPERVISOR

Describe your favorite boss or supervisor for us (temperament, techniques, outlook, etc.).

This is a good chance to find what the applicant responds favorably to in a supervisor. What qualities does he mention that he respected or grew to depend on? They may reflect his needs in a job situation. Did he value the supervisor's pep talks or incentive strategies, or was the attachment an emotional one, like the favorite teacher?

In describing his favorite boss, the applicant is responding positively to an authority figure. It may be significant if this question is conspicuously the only one he does not answer. In evaluating the response, look at where the boss appears in the applicant's history. If he cites his present boss, note which characteristics he mentions most positively and contrast them with why he wants to leave. What, particularly, does he respond to, and what does this tell you about his current needs for supervision? How, specifically, did the boss help him? How objective, articulate, and polished was the response?

The overachiever will value a person by the specific skills or knowledge he possesses. The entrepreneur appreciates management skills that he thinks he himself has acquired. He will also try to tell the interviewer what he wants to hear—standard virtues such as work dedication, honesty, and so on. The active will also appreciate people like himself—team players who are warm, funny, and enthusiastic in their dealings with him. The passive needs and values support and reinforcement. He will mention a person who was sensitive to, and tried to help him with, his problems. The aggressive type can be suspicious of other people's motives and feelings toward him. He will mention qualities without making a value judgment about them.

Overachiever

He is inclined to judge people in relation to task achievement, and the description of his favorite boss will tend to reflect this inclination: "Things were always clear with him; he really knew pension law and was always ready to work on a problem."

Entrepreneur

He admires most the supervisor who exhibits qualities that he believes he himself has: "Tom White. He knew the real world and how to work in it to make a buck. His tactics were completely pragmatic." Being pragmatic himself, he is likely to present in his description all the virtues he thinks you value, for example, "honest, economical, and hardworking." It is essential, therefore, to balance this response against his other responses.

Active

His answer will reflect his appreciation of warm, enthusiastic people: "John Johnson; he was straightforward, thoughtful, and supportive and included himself as part of the team."

Passive

People who provide support appeal to the passive person: "The boss I have now is interested in you as a person, not just as a worker; he really empathizes with your problems."

Aggressive

This person is basically insecure and somewhat suspicious of other people's motives toward him and will value someone who operates in the open: "Harry Harrison, because he speaks his mind and never holds a grudge; he lets you work on your own."

HARDEST SUPERVISOR

Tell us about the boss or supervisor that you found the hardest to work for (temperament, techniques, outlook, etc.).

In this response, the candidate may reflect what he fears in a job situation, a personality to which he reacts negatively, or his reaction to his own weaknesses. This question is difficult for many people to answer frankly; they dislike exhibiting negative feeling toward someone. What specific traits disturbed him, and is he projecting his own characteristics onto the boss? He may be revealing the anxieties he has in dealing with authority, as well as weaknesses he might have if he were put in charge. How sophisticated is his answer? Does he temper his criticism with some positive comment? He is reacting now to a past situation; are there signs that problem is still active in the applicant? Does he respect or dislike this boss? Does he list any positive qualities? Does he still seem to have this type of problem with people in his present life or job?

The overachiever is impatient with what he sees as incompetence. The active detests the slow and steady, while the entrepreneur dislikes people who enforce policies rooted in the past. The sensitized will find it hard to work for a supervisor who does not give him the individual attention and reinforcement he needs.

Entrepreneur

"He couldn't handle problems himself, and he was always caught up in past glories."

Active

"He was dull and noncreative and could only deal with one issue at a time; we even called him 'One-at-a-time Tom.'"

Passive

"He wouldn't talk to me on my level."

Sensitized

"He kept himself aloof and unreachable, showed no interest in my work, and made me feel unimportant."

POSITION MOST CAPABLE OF

For which jobs or posts would you be most capable? Please specify abilities or skills.

The list the applicant presents will reflect, of course, his own bias. Some people may include almost everything they have done, and such a response could indicate an applicant does not have the conviction that he can do anything particularly well. On the other hand, he might either be trying to cover all possible areas to make himself available for any job you might have or be obsessively concerned with giving a complete answer. Most will answer that their best qualifications fit the job for which they are applying. How reasonable is his answer? How complete is his answer, and how clearly was it expressed? Is his attention focused on the future, the present, or the recent or distant past?

You have to read between the lines of this answer to find clues about the applicant's behavior type.

Overachiever

"I feel securely qualified for management, considering the kind of work I've been called on to do in my present job."

Entrepreneur

"Sales. I'm doing well in that area right now; my commissions are really beginning to build."

Active

"I love the job I have now and feel I do it really well. I'd just like to do more of the same."

Aggressive

"I'd like a management position with my present company; I want to, and think I can, successfully lead others toward set goals."

ACCOMPLISHMENTS

Please describe a major work accomplishment (what, when, how).

Does he share credit for this accomplishment? Is it an actual accomplishment? Does this event show good problem-solving skills or merely luck? Look for evidence of managerial skills and qualities.

READING MATERIAL

What do you read on a regular basis?

This question is related to spare-time activities, like the next question. The overachiever will "barely have time for the newspaper" but may feel it necessary to read a variety of trade journals to make it in his field. The passive will answer almost identically, but his choice of journals will be more all-encompassing, providing him, for example, with financial advice and a light overview of world affairs. The entrepreneur will read biographies of people he admires as well as *Fortune, Money,* and *Wall Street Journal.* The sensitized will have a long list of reading material, but probably nothing that he reads regularly unless it relates to a specific interest. The compulsive will read generic magazines and some trade journals.

SPARE TIME

How do you spend your spare time? (sports or exercise, pastimes, clubs or groups, etc.). On the average, how much time do you allow for each in a normal week?

How the candidate uses his spare time will indicate how he will handle his job responsibilities. Do his activities indicate a need to be social or solitary? Is he a spectator or actual participant in these activities? Does he spend his spare time on hobbies or on improving some ability that he needs at work or that he simply feels he would like to develop? What use does the applicant make of available resources during his leisure time? Does he have hobbies, spend time with his family, or use his technical abilities? Do his avocations require an active or passive role? Which pursuits entail interacting with people and which require active involvement as opposed to being a spectator? This answer can also reveal how he deals with inevitable frustrations, setbacks, and so on.

Both the overachiever and the passive will feel that they have little or no spare time; this feeling is a function of the work ethic that is ingrained in their personality. It is simply their perception of their jobs. The sensitized pursues solitary activities like reading, music, or playing cards with small groups of people. The active may list many activities outside of, and unrelated to, work. One may attribute these to his youth or his lack of interest in his present position. The aggressive will tie in his activity with what he sees as an achievement, such as: "Lion's Club—just finished my term as president."

It is essential that this question be viewed in the context of the applicant's likely behavior type. For example, both the overachiever and the passive may claim to have little spare time because of the pressures of work, but this claim may be more a reflection of their perceptions than the actual situation.

Overachiever

"My job doesn't leave me much spare time."

Entrepreneur

"I enjoy watching professional sports and occasionally fit in some golf at the country club."

Active

This person will give a long list of activities. This could be attributed to youth or to a limited interest in his job.

Passive

"Most of my time and energy are taken up by my job."

Sensitized

"I read, play bridge, and am interested in photography and music."

Aggressive

"I'm a member of the Elks and am a past exalted ruler."

WORK-RELATED GROUPS

What work-related groups are you a member of? Please specify any offices that you hold or have held.

The kind of organizations to which individuals belong will reflect the interests that they have or the pressures they feel from work. Some individuals will join every work-related organization in an effort to feel more a part of their work environment. Do the organizations reflect a genuine enthusiasm for their work or a social interest (e.g., a national trade organization versus a specific company's Saturday luncheon discussion group)?

Notice the specific groups or organizations the applicant names. What indications do they give of his interests? The groups chosen may reveal his areas of stress or drive and may arise from a belief that they will gain him greater social recognition. Is the applicant involved with people, leadership, and responsibility? Can you see any pattern? Some people are not joiners; others may join many groups but give little commitment to any one group.

The entrepreneur will use these groups as networking opportunities, while the passive is not generally a joiner but will feel that his job will be in danger if he does not join a company organization. The active will hold a leadership position on the company softball team, but generally his social calendar will already be full. The sensitized will readily join only organizations that reflect his specific interests, which hopefully will overlap with his work (e.g., the Milton Society).

Overachiever

In general, the overachiever does not join clubs, but he might be involved in a religious or Sunday school activity. Of course, not all people who belong to church groups are overachievers, just consider this point within the context of other information.

Entrepreneur

This individual will list organizations related to business or civic duties (both of which he pursues with business objectives in mind), such as the National Association of Life Underwriters and the Junior Chamber of Commerce.

Active

He may list any number of organizations, depending on his work load and other outside commitments.

Passive

The passive individual may join a few organizations, but rarely as a leader. Frequently, his activities will be related to charity, and his answer may be something like, "I don't belong to any groups right now, but I do volunteer work at the puppet guild and for St. Vincent De Paul."

Sensitized

In general, if he belongs to any club or organization at all, it will be a specialized one that reflects a particular interest (e.g., American Association of Numismatists or Model Train Builders of the Southwest).

Aggressive

He will tend to record organizations in which he holds or held office (e.g., "sergeant at arms of the Lions Club; past grand knight in the Knights of Columbus").

WORK-RELATED CONFLICT

Please give us an example of a work-related conflict situation. What happened; who was involved; how was it resolved?

This response will be similar to the response to the "least favorite boss" question. Concern yourself with the source of the conflict. Does this conflict remain a problem with the candidate? Does it reflect an area of intolerance? Did the conflict involve an authority figure? Also note who receives credit for resolving the conflict or blame for the conflict in the first place.

CHILDHOOD INSPIRATION

As a youngster, did anyone inspire you to achieve your goals? Who, what did they do?

This answer will most likely reflect an authority figure from childhood, like the "influential teacher question" earlier. Look at how the individual is described. How did he inspire the candidate? What motives did his tactics appeal to? This information will be important to you as the prospective employer. Have the candidate's values changed? From the other responses, does the candidate feel that this type of encouragement is still valuable to him and his sense of self-worth?

SELF-IMAGE

How would you describe yourself today (how do you look at life, what do you like best about yourself and where are you not as strong, etc.)?

Observe precisely how this question is worded; it provides no structure or clues for the answer. Understanding how someone views himself significantly increases your ability to understand and predict his behavior. Keep in mind that the view presented is an edited account designed to emphasize positive traits and minimize negative ones. Also, people vary tremendously in their capability for self-examination and awareness, and this fact may affect the validity of the response.

The applicant may overplay qualities that are generally considered essential to good character, such as honesty and integrity. Careful attention should be paid to the first quality mentioned and the phrasing of the response, as these are highly significant. Summarize the response and then appraise carefully what was omitted, especially if you have clearly discerned these traits from other answers. What kind of style does he use in writing this description? Is it flat and unemotional, objective, restrained, expansive, confident, or impulsive? Are the stated characteristics really apt to be of consequence in his behavior? Is the image presented a real or an ideal one?

Remember that this description is presented from the perspective of the applicant's inherent way of viewing himself and the world. Consequently, producing 10 widgets per hour may seem underproductive to the overachiever, while producing 7 widgets per hour may seem like intolerable pressure to the high passive.

The overachiever will run down his list of hardworking, go-getter qualities, and perhaps add that he is a little impatient with others who are not as strong as he. The entrepreneur will project confidence in his abilities, his competitiveness, and his desire to succeed. The active will mention his affinity to people and will list as a weakness that he often does not spend enough time on important things because he has spread himself too thin. The passive will say that he is cautious and conscientious and tries to get things done right the first time. He will list good work-related qualities. The sensitized will be defending himself against the negative opinion he feels that the interviewer has formed. He will say that he likes himself, that he gets little satisfaction from his chosen career, and that he wishes he were more assertive. The aggressive will describe himself with qualities he admires. He sees himself as a natural leader and a go-getter.

This response should not be evaluated alone. Its reliable interpretation requires including and integrating the responses to the entire questionnaire.

Overachiever

"I'm disciplined, conscientious, and a hard worker. I enjoy people but sometimes find it hard to tolerate their imperfections."

Entrepreneur

"I'm ambitious and work hard to succeed; I'm competitive and confident in my own abilities; keeping track of details is not my strong point."

Active

"I enjoy being and working with people; I'm an optimist, a necessity in my business. I have to make time to be with my family more."

Sensitized

"I like myself. I know that I need to get along with people more to advance in the company, and I am working on this."

Aggressive

"I am very goal-oriented. In general I know where I am and where I want to be—and I will get there."

Compulsive

"I don't really know. But I do know I am organized and generally pleased with myself."

AMBITIONS

What would you like to accomplish in the future (goals, ambitions, projects, etc.)?

Goals and ambitions that are unrelated to the applicant's occupation may be included in evaluating this response. How realistic are the goals expressed, and how well defined are they? Are they expressions of career or other ambitions? Is his emphasis on social or on egocentric needs? How does his family fit in with his own personal aspirations? What does he fail to include? This omission can be as important as what he does include.

The overachiever will have work-related goals like the perfect sales force. The entrepreneur will wish for success to move on to something that he really wants to do that may seem frivolous to him now. The active will dream of having more time for the important things in his life. The passive will want to make his life better than his parents' and give his family security. Sensitized individuals wish for self-awareness and inner happiness. The aggressive type will mention typical middle-class values along with his desire for power and prestige.

Generally, applicants will concentrate on traditional, middle-class American goals, such as getting ahead, earning more money, accumulating status symbols, and so on, but sometimes they will disclose concerns or ideals that are expressions of their particular behavior type.

Overachiever

"I'd like to run an organization comprised of 10 self-disciplined, honest, and successful men who are highly knowledgeable and technically competent."

Entrepreneur

"My goal is to be a prosperous salesman, retire in 10 years, and then open a restaurant/bar in Aspen."

Active

"I want to spend more time with my wife and children."

Passive

"I want to avoid financial difficulties such as those my parents and sister have fallen into. I intend to make my family and myself financially secure."

Sensitized

"I'll be happy with peace of mind and self-fulfillment."

Aggressive

"I want to own a respectable home; have more children and earn a substantial income to support them and my wife; become prominent and influential in the government of my hometown; and become knowledgeable about my business so I can become one of the top men in my company."

GOAL RANKINGS

Rank the following goals in the order of importance for you. Give the highest a "1" and so on.

This question is among the most difficult to interpret. A particular behavior style does not always provide an obvious ranking. For example, the entrepreneur does not always rank wealth as his number one goal. The responses to these questions must be interpreted in light of the responses to the other questions.

SENTENCE COMPLETION

Please complete the following phrases to make sentences.

When Working with Others

Overachiever

"I try to be unbiased in my judgment and share equally in responsibilities."

"I work toward unity in a group and express my views without imposing them."

Entrepreneur

"I am able to see several points of view at once and like to know what motivates the people I'm working with."

"I most enjoy a situation where there's a balance between competition and fine-tuned teamwork."

Active

"I like working as part of a team and a feeling of close-knit oneness with my coworkers."

"I try to learn more about them and usually end up learning a lot about myself as well."

Passive

"I try to be cooperative and to get along with them by seeing their points of view."

"I'm generally uncomfortable and like to know what they think about the job we're doing."

Sensitized

"I like hearing what others think and enjoy the exchange of ideas."

"I myself find it hard to tell people my feelings, so I'm considerate of their likes and dislikes when they express them."

Aggressive

"I expect cooperation and everyone to do his share, although it's difficult sometimes to refrain from telling others how to do it."

"I want to be the leader and try to take command so the job gets done as quickly and as well as possible."

Compulsive

"I focus on my part of the job and try to be as organized about it as I can."

"I try to consider all the different opinions and approaches offered in fitting my own within the interests of the group and get a lot of satisfaction from accomplishing our task through cooperation."

I Work Best When

Overachiever

"I'm working on a concrete goal that urgently needs to be reached."

"I fully understand and value the objective and have been given the tools needed to get the job done."

Entrepreneur

"I have just had a great success and am faced with another challenge where I'm given free rein."

"I'm under some pressure and completing the job will result in some reward, such as more money."

Active

"I deal with people, perhaps addressing large groups of them, and am involved in fast-paced activity."

"I enjoy the work I'm doing and the atmosphere and surroundings are pleasant."

Passive

"I'm comfortable with the people and surroundings and feel confident about what I am doing."

"I can rely on my company while I work at improving my skills."

Sensitized

"I'm given instructions and then allowed to assume the responsibility of getting the job done on my own."

"I'm inspired and/or relaxed."

Aggressive

"I'm not under pressure and am in a position that's important to getting something I believe in done."

"I'm given broad guidance but allowed to work without direct supervision."

Compulsive

"I'm working on a well-defined project with a minimum of distractions."

"Everything is neatly organized and I feel confident."

What People Don't Like About Me

Overachiever

"is I'm working hard to get ahead, willing to put in the long hours required, and leaving my old job and coworkers behind."

"is I'm a perfectionist and at times exacting and precise."

Entrepreneur

"is my irritation with small talk and my talking about my successes."

"not much, if anything."

Active

"is I talk fast and maybe too much."

"is my extreme enthusiasm and excitement about life."

Passive

"is the things I say and do and probably the way I dress sometimes, which bothers me."

"is that I'm not witty and fun."

Sensitized

"is my restraint, quietness, and seeming aloofness."

"is my tendency to take things too seriously at times and to be independent in my thinking."

Aggressive

"is that I'm inclined to speak my mind bluntly, even when not asked my opinion or when my opinion differs from the group's."

"is I'm somewhat domineering and quick to lose my temper."

Compulsive

"is I tend to be analytical and dogmatic and work too hard with an obsessive need to complete a job in all its details."

"is I have little patience at times for the poor performance of others if I know they have received proper instructions."

When I'm Not Doing Something Well

Overachiever

"I step back and analyze the problem to find another way to do it better."

"I find out what I'm doing wrong and then study or practice until I've got it right."

Entrepreneur

"I know it right away but never get anxious or give up."

"I realize it's because I'm not using my intelligence and am somehow hindering myself."

Active

"I get blocked and lose my initiative for the project."

"I leave it for a while and either do another project or get a change of scenery for a few minutes and then tackle it again."

Passive

"I need someone to let me know and then show me in an encouraging way how to do better."

"I'm unhappy, frustrated, and upset with myself."

Sensitized

"I might set it aside briefly to allow a more creative approach to surface in my mind or try to isolate and analyze the problem for a better solution."

"it's because I've been lost in my own little dream world."

Aggressive

"I get irritated with myself because I know I can do better."

"I stop and start again."

Compulsive

"I stop to analyze the situation and plan for ways to improve what I am doing."

"I ask for suggestions and recommendations for improvement from others."

I Want to

Overachiever

"be a good husband and father and succeed at my career goals."

"be excellent at whatever I do."

Passive
"get into a secure work position."
"have people like me and have someone love me and be with me."

Sensitized
"be in harmony with myself and content with my life."
"be an inspiration to my children and see them better themselves."

Compulsive
"be highly efficient at my job and be proud of my performance."
"do the best I can with the talents I have."

My Best Trait Is

Active
"my ability to get along with people and my willingness to communicate."
"I try to be open-minded and sensitive to others while being a good listener."

Passive
"I'm dependable and listen to others' opinions."
"I agree with most people and try to be positive."

Aggressive
"I'm persistent and determined."
"I'm confident in what I know and am willing to teach it to others."

Compulsive
"I apply myself to a job and become deeply involved in it."
"my ability to stick with a job and make sure it gets done, no matter what."

People Like Me Best for

Entrepreneur
"the way I put people at ease and make them feel important."
"the drive I have and the confident, smooth way I operate."

Passive
"my sincerity and dependability, I hope."
"my personality, I guess."

Aggressive
"my honesty and candidness."
"my leadership abilities and empathy for others."

Compulsive

"my organized and thorough way of working."

"being an honest and hard worker who can be counted on to get the job done."

I Find It Difficult to

Overachiever

"accept failure in myself, my friends, or associates."

"be content with mediocrity."

Active

"understand why people are not always cooperative, resolute in doing their best, and positive in outlook."

"be idle."

Aggressive

"keep my opinions to myself when I know I'm right."

"tolerate bigoted people or to have to train men and women older than 40."

Sensitized

"express my feelings in words, to start a conversation with a stranger."

"accept people's insensitivity to things like poverty and hunger, when there are so many resources and so much information available."

What Most Makes Me Feel Good Is

Entrepreneur

"making a big sale and getting the income from it."

"competing in a hard-fought contest and coming out knowing I've done my best."

Sensitized

"spending time with someone special and sharing ideas with intelligent people."

"spending quiet time thinking and appreciating nature."

Aggressive

"seeing someone I've helped succeed, whether an employee whom I've helped train or someone outside of work."

"getting promotions my peers don't get."

Compulsive

"working hard and knowing I've done my job thoroughly and the best I can."

"when I've helped an employee improve his skills and performance."

I Close Up When

Overachiever

"I'm working with people who are incompetent or who don't put in enough effort."

"I have to work on something that serves no useful purpose."

Entrepreneur

"I'm held on a close rein and constantly have to report to my supervisor."

"someone insists I do something his way."

Sensitized

"I'm in a large group of people I don't know, particularly if some of them are offensive or overbearing."

"I'm involved in conversations that conflict with my own beliefs and thoughts."

Aggressive

"I'm in a situation where I can't use my abilities."

"my boss is insecure and fearful of allowing me to grow and show my merit."

Being Secure Means

Overachiever

"being able to trust your own feelings and ideas and being confident of doing the best you know how."

"having a clear sense of purpose in your life, in both personal and career areas."

Sensitized

"feeling centered in myself and having the peace of mind that comes from that."

"having what I need to live: food, housing, clothing, a good companion to share them with, and a close relationship with God."

Aggressive

"being in a good, financially rewarding position and knowing your family is well provided for."

"having confidence in who you are and what you can do."

Compulsive

"I have the abilities and information necessary to do my job well."

"being able to rely only on myself and my ability to work hard to succeed."

I Get Excited When

Overachiever

"I know I've done the job well and reached the goal I was aiming for."

"I see someone achieve a goal."

Entrepreneur

"I conceive of a plan of action that will result in my getting wealthy."

"I'm in control of a situation and finish first."

Passive

"someone confronts me with the upsetting news that I've done something wrong."

"someone compliments me and likes me."

Aggressive

"I'm getting ready for a big sale."

"I see a well-played athletic event."

People I Like Least

Active

"have negative outlooks."

"have closed minds and are prejudiced."

Passive

"are arrogant, pretentious, and insensitive to other people's feelings."

"are ruthless and cynically take advantage of people."

Aggressive

"are unambitious and do nothing to better themselves."

"always whine and make excuses and have no self-respect."

Compulsive

"are people who boast too much about themselves and are phony."

"are those who use devious manipulation instead of dealing with me honestly."

I Most Like My

Active

"positive attitude toward life and ability to do a variety of things well."

"freedom of movement in my sales job."

Sensitized

"development as a person; the way I've worked to realize my potential."

"minister: he's offered me a model on which to build my own life."

Aggressive

"ability to manage and instruct people, either individually or by speaking to large groups."

"dynamic personality and ability to hold my own."

Compulsive

"ability to look at a difficult job, pinpoint the problems, and break them down into understandable and manageable parts."

"feeling of satisfaction after I've finished a job quickly and efficiently."

I Like Having a Lot of Time for

Overachiever

"developing and improving myself."

"finishing projects that need finishing."

Active

"engaging in social activities where I meet and talk with people."

"my hobbies or doing other things I enjoy, such as travel and recreation."

Passive

"appraising all my alternatives when I have a problem."

"rest and contemplation, especially after a hard day at the office."

Aggressive

"outdoor activities, such as hunting, fishing, and skiing."

"pursuing a rewarding career."

When Depressed I

Overachiever

"remind myself that everyone gets depressed at times and then get myself out of it through self-motivation."

"involve myself in something interesting."

Entrepreneur

"get physically active and play some intense sport, like racquetball."

"get away from the reason, fast."

Passive

"need to be with friends who will cheer me up."

"withdraw from people, get quiet, and cry."

Compulsive

"remind myself it won't last and get involved in something constructive."

"need either to deal with the problem causing it or put my energy into some other productive activity."

When by Myself

Entrepreneur

"I make money-making plans and think about what my next move should be."

"I enjoy it because I'm in good company."

Active

"I either spend the time at something actively productive—perhaps something good for my health—or rest completely."

"I enjoy it because I have many things I can do that interest me."

Passive

"I tend to worry about problems and remember lost time and opportunities."

"I think of others and like to pray for them."

Sensitized

"I am able to relax because there are no outside distractions."

"I spend my time thinking, reading, listening to music, and generally just enjoying my own company."

Sometimes I

Overachiever

"take time to think about my objectives, sometimes readjusting them in the light of new circumstances."

"feel the drive to achieve something exceptional in my life."

Sensitized

"enjoy moments alone or just watching people."

"get ideas and inspirations for things I'd like to do."

Aggressive

"jump the gun and try things before I'm really prepared for them."

"want to move in and show people how I can help them."

Compulsive

"work too hard and try to do everything myself."

"get a clearer perspective on a problem by letting it go for a while and then going back to it."

4

Preparing for the Interview

This chapter highlights the importance of adequate preparation for an interview. A properly conducted interview represents an opportunity for the interviewer both to meet and evaluate a candidate and to advertise something about the company that he represents. Adequate preparation can ensure that the interviewer maintains a perceptive eye while interviewing candidates and projects the right impression of his company.

First and foremost, the interviewer should recognize the necessity of being prepared. The effect of a prepared interviewer on a candidate is similar to that of a prepared teacher on a group of students. Almost no matter what grade a student receives from a prepared teacher, he is more inclined to think that it was fair. Similarly, most candidates will feel fairly treated if they perceive that the interviewer is prepared for their meeting.

In contrast, unprepared interviews are frequently inadequate and can have negative consequences for both the interviewer and the candidate. If the interviewer is not adequately prepared when meeting the candidate, then he is advertising something negative about himself and the company. Moreover, an unprepared interviewer will not be as effective in reading the candidate or in presenting his company in the best possible light. A candidate who is interviewed by an unprepared interviewer and is subsequently rejected for a position may have a legitimate case for an EEOC complaint.

This chapter is organized to remind the interviewer of some simple, easily overlooked, but critical steps to preparing for every interview. These steps are briefly discussed as a preparation for reviewing the process of interviewing.

The interview is over, and you do not have enough information to decide if the prospective employee is the person to fill the position. Or interview time is up, and you must end before having asked about important areas in the person's background. Or you have finished the interview and are left with the feeling that you lost control of the dialogue. Have you ever had these experiences?

If you have encountered any of these situations, you have something in common with most interviewers.

Thorough and careful preparation and planning are the most constructive and effective ways to avoid these and other common interviewing pitfalls. By having a clear idea of what you are trying to assess and a clear plan for how you will get the information you need, you will increase substantially your ability to control the interview efficiently and to complete it with sufficient information to make a legitimate decision.

PRELIMINARY GROUNDWORK

It is absolutely essential that you know exactly what you are seeking before you even contemplate doing an interview. Generalized objectives like "The position requires a strong technical background and an ability to work well with other people" are of limited value and may actually mislead.

This whole process may be understood and appreciated better by a quick review of the different parts of the SKAP profile. The formal job analysis that a SKAP profile provides to the interviewer defines the crucial components of particular positions. This analysis is often provided by personnel specialists in large organizations; if such a resource is not available to you, it is your responsibility as the interviewer to secure this information. One useful approach is to consider what the position requirements are in the four distinct SKAP areas: (1) skill, (2) knowledge, (3) aptitude, and (4) personal characteristics.

The skill requirements for a given position should be defined as explicitly as possible. It is important to evaluate the specific skills demanded by a particular position. For instance, a machine operator may be required to set up and run a 10-ton press but may not be required to troubleshoot mechanical breakdowns; project management skills may or may not be necessary for a particular technical or engineering position. Try to be as specific as possible in defining the skills required.

As an example, an effective description of the typing and shorthand skills required for a secretarial position would be that one (1) must type a minimum of 50 words per minute with no errors and (2) must take shorthand at a minimum of 80 words per minute. Defining the exact skills necessary for success in a particular position, however, is beyond the scope of the book. For example, the book does not provide specific information on interviewing for the technical skills involved in engineering, accounting, or finance.

The knowledge required by a position depends greatly on the various capacities in which the candidate must function. A secretary who must function as receptionist, purchasing agent, and minutes secretary will have knowledge vastly different from that of a paralegal or laboratory clerk. There are also differences in the knowledge requirements of different types of salesmen; selling farm equipment requires an entirely different frame of reference than does the sale of stocks and bonds. If the interviewer expects his managerial staff to interact regularly with factory workers and clients, he must look for the knowledge and frame of reference to provide this function.

The aptitude portion of a job description often includes a discussion of the mental abilities required to perform the job function. For example, a position as a computer programmer may require a college degree in some scientific field like engineering, math, or computer science. But the position may also require the aptitude to write computer code in a very efficient manner. This aptitude can be assessed with specific mental tests. Some positions, like fireman, may require the physical aptitude to lift and carry a human body a distance of 50 feet; a candidate's aptitude to perform this physical feat can also be effectively tested.

The personal characteristics are often the most difficult to explore during the interview process. What are the personal characteristics that the candidate must have? Not only are personal characteristics harder to define than knowledge or skills, but it is often more difficult to demonstrate how they are related to a particular job. A large part of this book is devoted to the assessment of personal characteristics, like competitive drive, emotional energy, enthusiasm, high goal orientation, and dynamic sales presence.

Obviously some overlap exists among the four SKAP factors. That is, as a rule, a candidate with a significant amount of mental aptitude but limited specific knowledge of a given topic can probably learn new material very quickly. In this way, the four SKAP factors are considered complementary and provide relative benchmarks for rating a given candidate on a particular SKAP factor for a specific position. For example, the position description for an entry-level computer programmer position may read: "A person should have either a college degree in computer science [knowledge] or a very high amount of abstract reasoning aptitude [aptitude]."

In general, the traditional SKAP profile is a very effective way to measure the requirements needed for managerial and sales positions. This book assumes that a SKAP profile has been compiled for a given position and that specific position requirements, like social persuasiveness, leadership, competitive drive, coaching, judgment, and knowledge to read people, have been included in the profile. The book will not individually categorize any of these position requirements as a separate skill, knowledge, ability, or personal characteristic but will jointly summarize them as interpersonal skills. So, any job requirement dealing with people will be defined as an interpersonal skill. This book is designed to help you measure interpersonal skills during the interview process.

PREPARING FOR AN INTERVIEW
WITH A SPECIFIC CANDIDATE

The next step is to start planning for a specific interview. You may want to create your own method of planning the interview, but it is advisable that you include the following eight steps:

Chart 4.1
Position Analysis Chart

	Low				Medium	High		
	– – – – – – – – –				5	+ + + + + + + +		
Overachiever								
Entrepreneur								
Active								
Passive								
Sensitized								
Aggressive								
Compulsive								

Step 1: Review the SKAP Analysis

Remember to focus on the personal characteristics (interpersonal skills) required by the position. Chart 4.1 is designed to assist you.

Consider the type and degree of interpersonal skills the job requires. Are you looking for a disciplined but competitive individualist who strives to win sales contests? Or are you seeking a senior-level general manager who is disciplined but personable, friendly, and sociable but who is also capable of being domineering and aggressive and readily takes a position of leadership among the sales/manufacturing/administrative personnel? The first scenario suggests someone who is high on the entrepreneurial trait. The second description might be a person who is high on the active and aggressive traits. The assumption is that both of these individuals need relatively high scores on the overachiever trait.

Let's mark the chart above for a generic sales position. Take a pencil and mark the level of each of the seven traits discussed in chapter 2 that you think a generic sales position requires. This process will help you keep clear in your mind the judgments you will be called on to make after the interview.

Save your rankings on this chart because we will compare them to rankings for the candidate on a similar chart later.

Step 2: Examine Related Written Material

This material will certainly include the 120 Questionnaire. It may also include other application and personal history forms, resumes, letters of recommendation, reference checks, comments from previous interviews in the company, and so on. Let's review some written material from a sample candidate situation. This review will enable us to measure our understanding of the material presented thus far in the book and provide a platform for additional material. The sample candidate situation includes the following: (1) position fact sheet, (2) candidate resume, and (3) candidate responses to the 120 Questionnaire.

POSITION FACT SHEET

Job Title: Sales Representative, Financial (Insurance) Products
SKAP Analysis: College degree or equivalent work experience.

> Position requires interacting primarily with middle-upper income, college-educated adults, and college-educated are generally more successful than others in the position.

Some (2–5 years) selling experience.

> Position requires knowledge of selling techniques and methods. Should have completed sales training course(s) and generally be aware of methods of presenting features, benefits, and advantages of a given product.

Works independently.

> Some supervision, but prefer a person who works best with minimal supervision. After brief training will have weekly follow-up meetings during which he presents results.

Motivated by commission selling.

> Compensation package includes reasonable base and significant incentive compensation. Bonus is available if production is sufficient.

Socially persuasive.

> Some "cold calling" required. Person must be able to take rejection and quickly rebound to make the next call with a positive frame of reference.

Highly energetic.

> Some Saturday meetings and overnight (weekend) travel may be required. Must possess the energy to do this.

Some knowledge of financial products.

> Will train to some degree, but prefer someone with at least a speaking knowledge of stocks and bonds and a National Association of Securities Dealers (NASD) license.

Setting: Today's date: December 1, 1989
Location: Philadelphia, PA
Salary range: Base $27,500–$42,500; Incentives up to additional $25,000.

CANDIDATE RESUME

Sam "Mickey" Johnson
222 E. 68th Street
New York, NY 10020

Age: 30+
Health: Excellent
Marital Status: Single

Objective

To locate a position that allows for maximum use of my developing sales/marketing talents and that will reward me with increasing levels of individual responsibility in an atmosphere of achievement.

Work History

Prudential/Bache Securities, New York City
Sales representative
9/87–11/89
Sale of securities and financial equity products.

Xerox Office Supplies, Stamford, CT
Account representative
9/85–6/87
Sale of office systems (including copiers, minicomputers, typewriters, etc.). Number one salesman in the region, 3d and 4th quarters 1986.

Education

Thunderbird School of Management, Tempe, AZ
M.B.A.: International business, 9/83–6/85
Southern Methodist University: Dallas, TX
B.A.: History, 9/77–6/82

Other

Preparatory studies: Choate Academy
President and social chairman of fraternity in college
Active in SMU Alumni Association
Outside interests include squash, European skiing, and sailing

CANDIDATE RESPONSES TO THE 120 QUESTIONNAIRE

120 Q: Describe your development. What factors (family, education, work, etc.) influenced you to be the person that you are today?

120 A: I was raised in a financially comfortable but demanding environment. My parents expected us to act independently and to achieve a series of meaningful goals—high school activities, college, and gainful employment. I have enjoyed my first two full-time employment positions but have not yet reached my potential.

120 Q: Did you interrupt or fail to finish any level of your education? If so, please explain.

120 A: Yes, I left college after my sophomore year and "explored life" for a while. I went to Europe for three months, drove a cab in NYC for a while (lived in the Village), and finally moved home for the summer. Then I returned to school.

120 Q: What kind of work would you enjoy doing 5 years from now? How much would you want to earn then?

120 A: I see myself as a salesman. I know my own strengths and weaknesses reasonably well, and sales is the place for me. Given this, I think selling "money," some kind of financial product, makes the most sense to me. The commissions are higher, and the rewards are greater. In terms of income I see myself making around $200,000+ per year in five years, (today's dollars).

120 Q: As a youngster did anyone inspire you to achieve your goals? Who, what did they do?

120 A: Yes, my grandfather. He lived to be 80 years old and was going into his office almost until the day he died. He was always kind to me but he was a difficult taskmaster to others. Although he was willing to pay a day's wage for a day's work, he demanded that day's work from anyone he hired.

120 Q: I feel that money

120 A: is important.

120 Q: Working on fine points

120 A: is necessary but can frequently be delegated.

Step 3: Make Note of Questions About Any Incomplete, Curious, or Confusing Items

For example, if the candidate conveyed that he left an earlier position for "a better opportunity," you might ask what prospects were lacking and whether or not his next job did provide these prospects.

In the example of Sam "Mickey" Johnson, some items are worth noting. For instance:

1. Why does he list his age as 30+? Is he being "cute"? Is he saying that he has reached a certain minimal age of maturity? Is he indicating a general dislike for detailed information? Is he baiting the potential interviewer for a potential EEOC age issue? We are not interested in his exact age for any purpose of discrimination; we are curious about his form of communication and what it can tell us about him.

2. He apparently likes to use the nickname of "Mickey." Does this single item suggest any behavior trait? Using a nickname is fine, and it also provides an easy entry piece of information about which to start a conversation with him. For example, the interviewer can ask, "Should I call you Sam, or do most people call you Mickey?" This question shows the candidate that you read his material and took notice of his highlighting his name.

3. He apparently spent five years completing college, 9/77–6/82. Does he think that taking the year off in Europe, driving a cab in New York City, and finally returning home for the summer helped him develop or mature emotionally? What evidence can he offer that he did mature as a result of this year-off experience?

4. The time between college graduation (6/82) and the beginning of his M.B.A. program (9/83) is not accounted for on the resume. What did he do (professional employment, vacation, summer jobs, and so on) between 6/82 and 9/83? Does he think this was not worth mentioning? If so, what else is not worth mentioning?

5. How did he get the job at Xerox? Answer a classified ad? Family connections? Alumni association? What does his answer suggest about his personal ambition?

6. He was apparently raised in the East but attended college in Texas and completed an M.B.A. in Arizona. Why did he attend undergraduate school in Texas? Why the M.B.A.? Why in Arizona? How and why does a major in international business lead to a career interest in sales?

7. He attended private (expensive) schools but makes no mention of scholarships, loans, and expenses. How was his education financed? How did he perform academically? Although many studies show the lack of relationship between academic performance and later success, the answer to these questions can give some indication of his self-discipline, interests, and behavior traits. Was he too busy with social activities to emphasize his academic training?

8. He indicates a goal of an income of $200,000 five years hence. Is this realistic? Does he have an objective plan to accomplish this stated goal? For some people such goals may be realistic, but based on the information available, this figure for him suggests more an unrealistic wish than an objective goal. Again, this suggests a partial trait pattern of high entrepreneur with low overachiever.

9. He indicates that his health is "excellent" and his marital status is "single." You may acknowledge the health statement, but not the marital status information. Obviously it is impossible to ignore the written information, but do not raise the issue during the interview and, of course, ignore it when considering his candidacy. Marital information is not relevant to job qualifications. A candidate may be trying subtly to indicate to any prospective employer that he is free to travel and more inclined to work extra hours. For whatever reason he included the information, however, it should be disregarded as part of the interview process.

Step 4: Organize and Record Your Initial Impressions

Use the Candidate Analysis Chart (Chart 4.2) to chart your impressions from the information you have. These are preliminary ideas, subject to modification upon further exploration during the interview. Review the position fact sheet, candidate resume, and candidate sample responses to the 120 Questionnaire. Can you draw any tentative conclusions from them? Can you identify any topic areas that need additional exploration in the interview? Do you have some (even vague) impressions of the candidate? To the extent

Chart 4.2
Candidate Analysis Chart

	Low			Medium		High	
	- - - - - - - - -			5		+ + + + + + +	
Overachiever							
Entrepreneur							
Active							
Passive							
Sensitized							
Aggressive							
Compulsive							

possible, using the information above, fill in the Candidate Analysis Chart for Mr. Sam "Mickey" Johnson.

Obviously, this task is not easy. You have received limited definitions of the traits mentioned above, and you also have no training in terms of what the ratings ($- - -5+ + +$) represent in actual behavior. For example, "How much overachiever behavior does a ranking of $- -5$ or $5+ +$ represent?" is a legitimate question at this point.

Please try, however, to fill in the chart. In general, without any knowledge of a person, assume that he ranks a 5 (a middle-range score in terms of the chart) on every trait. Then review the written material about him and try to move his ranking up or down ($5+ +$ or $- -5$), based on your impressions of his written material. Make notes of both your ranking and your reasoning for each rank. For example, under entrepreneur you might rank him $5+ +$ and write in partial support of that ranking; for example, his references to the importance of money as an entity.

With only the information available about the candidate so far it is difficult to gain a valid picture of him. He would probably be ranked $5+$ on the entrepreneurial, active, and aggressive traits. He would probably be ranked 5 on the overachiever trait. He would be ranked -5 on the passive, sensitized, and compulsive traits. Why?

These judgments are largely intuitive but are based on some well-researched evidence. These rankings are preliminary and can be changed when meeting the candidate in person.

He appears to have been raised in a financially comfortable environment and to have been somewhat indulged in his upbringing. Also, he attended an exclusive and expensive prep school. His undergraduate and M.B.A. educations were both at private schools (without mention of academic distinction or scholarship awards), presumably away from home at increased expense. He currently lives in an expensive part (the so-called Upper East Side) of New York City, and this requires money, an appreciation for a status-conscious address, or likely both. His year off from school (between sophomore and junior years) was spent in Europe and driving a cab, not especially demanding positions, nor do they suggest much idealism or social service. This information suggests that he is somewhat narcissistic and probably socially polished in his demeanor.

He sees himself as being very worthwhile and is in the business of selling himself first and whatever product he happens to represent second. His self-description comments from the 120 Questionnaire that he sees himself as a salesman, that he knows his strengths and weaknesses, and that he sees himself making $200,000+ per year in five years all suggest that he is money-motivated, perhaps somewhat self-indulged, and accustomed to a comfortable living style. None of these self-descriptors is necessarily good or bad; however, they do help us describe him with a set of behavior traits. In fact, many very successful salespeople would describe themselves in the same manner. His entrepreneur instincts are fully developed; he would easily rank a 5+ on this trait.

He appears to be politely sociable but primarily money-motivated. He was social chairman and president of his college fraternity and is currently active in the alumni association. He probably uses the nickname Mickey frequently and likes people to remember him as a friendly and personable individual. He may well be socially comfortable with others and projects a certain social charm and personal vitality. Hence, his active ranking is 5+.

He is competitive but not especially self-disciplined. His idea of a demanding environment is to complete high school with some activities, finish college, and get a job. His overachiever ranking is difficult to measure. True, he does not obviously show an overabundance of self-discipline, but he may possess a reasonable amount of it. He is competitive and money-motivated, but he has experienced some success in sales, which takes discipline. Moreover, his professional employment track record (two years with each employer) will have to be reviewed for evidence of growth and success.

The passive trait reflects some degree of caution or personal moodiness. No signs of this trait are readily available. He may be perceptive in reading people—the entrepreneur frequently is—but he does not seem especially shy or introverted about meeting others. The passive person needs, wants, and at times demands time to check his impressions of a situation and refine his thinking about a given topic. He needs to ensure that he is right before making a recommendation. Mickey Johnson shows little inclination for such behavior.

Moreover, the sensitized person needs time for reflection and likes being alone to recharge his emotional batteries to face the ordeal of interacting with people in a social setting. Again, this description does not appear to match Mickey's more sociable manner. Hence, the −5 ranks on the sensitized and passive traits. His indication that details can frequently be delegated suggests a lack of concern for details and a preference for not working with them; hence, the −5 compulsive score.

We have reached some tentative but fairly strong conclusions based on limited information about the candidate. The information presented, however, is obviously slanted but not atypical for a position in sales. Moreover, it is assumed that the remainder of the information about Mickey is consistent with the information presented; then the conclusions presented would be more obvious. The reader is warned, however, against developing too firm a mental set before seeing the candidate. It is critical to keep an open mind when interviewing the individual. But just as an experienced interviewer uses a resume to make some basic decisions on which candidates to interview, it is suggested here that some preliminary charts can be drawn to describe a candidate's behavior traits before he is actually interviewed.

Based on this information alone, how does he match the requirements of the Position Analysis Chart? Does he appear to fit sufficiently well so that he should be interviewed further? At this stage, he probably fits reasonably well for an additional interview.

Step 5: Remind Yourself of the Importance of Not Asking Some Particular Questions

This unusual-sounding step is an important segment of preparing for the interview. It is critically important to be aware of the questions not to ask during the interview. This book is not described as a legal primer on the issue of fair employment interviewing. Other texts deal with this issue exclusively, and you may well wish to consider one of them for specific details on this topic. The book does, however, try to make you aware of the importance of this issue. The topic can be confusing, frustrating, and expensive. In general, the book suggests a commonsense approach to the topic. Let's begin by reviewing the following questions.

Please read each of the following questions carefully. Mentally mark an X by each question that is not allowed to be in an interview for a position with your company.

_____ 1. Are you married?

_____ 2. That's an interesting name. What nationality is it?

_____ 3. Have you ever been arrested?

_____ 4. I see you speak French. Is English your native language?

_____ 5. How old is your youngest child?

_____ 6. Are you a member of the Knights of Columbus?

_____ 7. Would you get your hair cut if you got this job?

_____ 8. What do you think of women's lib?

_____ 9. Are you a regular churchgoer?

_____ 10. Have you ever been convicted of a crime?

It may be surprising or obvious to you that under most circumstances, each of the questions above should have an X by it. That is, generally speaking, for most employment interviews, each of the above questions is a violation of the law, and asking them can subject you and your company to an EEOC investigation.

Again, as a rule common sense is often a good guide. Ask questions that are directly related to the SKAP profile that defined the position. Certainly you are allowed and encouraged to ask questions that relate to a person's interpersonal skills for working effectively with others. You are not allowed, however, to pry needlessly into the private life of a person and ask questions that are not related to the requirements of the position.

Avoid questions that deal with information about topics such as age, race, ancestry, sex, or ethnic group. The importance of avoiding direct questions about these topics is obvious, but an interviewer can subtly make mistakes in this area. For example, if the candidate lists membership in a religiously oriented social group (Knights of Columbus, Temple Union Group, Baptists Support Group), you may mentally note a group membership, but you should not delve further into the nature of association with this group unless it is clearly job-related.

Avoid asking questions of a particular group of candidates that you would not ask all candidates. For example, you cannot ask a married woman, "Who will take care of the children when you have sales meetings and weekend travel?" unless you are prepared to ask the same question of the married men who are candidates for the position. In the same way, you should not ask a married woman, "How would your husband feel about the overnight travel requirements of the position?" unless you are prepared to ask the men how their wives will feel about such travel. It is best to ask neither question of either group.

Sexual discrimination is probably the most sensitive area in employment interviewing. This is both illegal and ineffective as an increasing number of women prove their worth at the managerial and executive levels of many corporations. Women rightfully occupy an increasing number of positions at the managerial level of an organization. To some extent, however, expectations and biases may exist among interviewers when reviewing women who aspire to higher-level managerial positions in any organization. Women who aspire to such higher levels can be perceived as socially aggressive, while men are classified as being achievement-oriented. Women may be described as sexy, while men are considered socially polished, but clearly the description of polish can apply to both sexes. So it is important to avoid male/female stereotypes and focus on the requirements of the position.

Racial discrimination is another sensitive issue. Some ethnic groups may be unfairly described as being less reliable or stable than others and therefore unfit as a group for the position. Moreover, those minority personnel who are selected are assumed to be part of a quota or a result of tokenism. This assumption is an invalid classification of people and a legally unfair employment consideration. Nonetheless, some interviewers may need to be educated to reevaluate their own racial stereotypes. Further, avoid asking questions about any minority groups or social issues associated with them.

Religious discrimination is also a topic that needs to be mentioned. Some interviewers tend to feel that a candidate who shares their own religious background is automatically a better candidate. Conversely, the further away the candidate's religion is from the interviewer's religion, the less desirable that particular candidate becomes. This attitude is fundamentally flawed and ineffective. If used as a hiring criterion, it is illegal in interviewing candidates. During the interview process it is wise to avoid questions about church attendance, church-related groups, or the religious aspects of a candidate's education. For example, some colleges (like the University of Notre Dame) are both well known and generally associated with a particular religion. You may ask about the college experience in general but not about any religious affiliation or training received as a result of attending such schools.

Finally, dealing with sensitive questions about the company policies on EEOC issues is an important issue. If the questions are presented to you in a socially aggressive manner, do not get caught up in the candidate's emotionality. Use common sense and avoid saying anything stupid. Mentally take a deep breath and, if true, be willing to say, "I don't know what our policy is about X. But I will be happy to investigate it and get back to you." In general, however, if you are involved in the interview process, you should have some knowledge of your company's EEOC policies and procedures.

Step 6: Know Yourself

This simple-sounding homily is important and critical to the interview itself. It is mentioned as part of the preparation stage to remind you simply to take a few moments to be aware of your own idiosyncracies, possible biases, and frames of reference in interviewing candidates. Do not necessarily use yourself as a model for the position you are trying to fill. Think in terms of the SKAP profile, not your personal needs and perceptions of the job. Think about the job requirements and be objective in evaluating a person's strengths and weaknesses, in terms of interpersonal skills, in meeting those requirements.

Chart 4.3
Personal Analysis Chart

	Low			Medium 5		High	
	- - - - - - - - -			5	+ + +	+ + + +	
Overachiever							
Entrepreneur							
Active							
Passive							
Sensitized							
Aggressive							
Compulsive							

One convenient way to start the process of knowing yourself is simply to rank yourself on the seven behavior traits. If necessary, review the material presented that describes and defines the traits and then try to rank yourself on the traits. Chart 4.3, the Personal Analysis Chart, is presented to help you in this process.

By briefly charting yourself, you can gain some insight into your own strengths and potential weaknesses in terms of interviewing the candidate. Most people, consciously or not, tend to assume that other people either are or should be like themselves. Hence, they frequently interview and recommend candidates who appear to have trait patterns similar to their own patterns. More experienced interviewers are generally aware of their own biases and will work to correct for them during the interview process.

If you, for example, ranked yourself high on the overachiever and active traits, chances are you will be looking to select someone with a similar trait pattern. Similar biases are also a function of our work group orientation. For example, many companies use multi-interviewing techniques. In this situation managers from different areas interview candidates for each other's departments; the manager of administration may interview a candidate for a position in the sales department.

In terms of the Personal Analysis Chart the manager of administration may rank himself $5+++$ on the overachiever, compulsive, and sensitized traits; $5+$ on the active and passive traits; 5 on the aggressive trait; and $--5$ on the entrepreneur trait. The Position Analysis Chart (following the SKAP profile) suggests that a highly entrepreneurial-aggressive trait pattern would be successful in the position. Such a candidate is currently interviewing for the position. The initial reaction of the manager of administration to the candidate may be that he is not suited for the position. His primary, although unspoken reason is that the candidate's interpersonal skills (high entrepreneur-aggressive) are not similar to those of himself (the manager of administration).

This description may be slanted, but this type of situation does occur in the interviewing process and highlights the need for any interviewer to be systematically aware of his own trait pattern and the effect this can have on his perception of a candidate. This awareness will enable him to understand better his own preferences or biases in selecting personnel, separate these preferences from the job requirements, and hence make more effective selection recommendations for the organization.

Step 7: Arrange the Questions in a Logical Sequence

To proceed smoothly with the interview, order your questions in some rational sequence. It may be helpful to prepare a separate sheet for each major background area you plan to cover in the interview, for example, work history, education, work-related outside activities, other. It is simple then to write down on a single page all questions that, for example, relate to work history, regardless of the trait to which they are directed.

You will need to include all of the candidate's background in your interview, but, obviously, some areas are of more importance than others. There are no hard-and-fast rules about how much emphasis and time should be given to any particular area. Much of what you decide will hinge on the background and experience of a particular candidate. In most circumstances, a major portion of the time should be devoted to a review of the candidate's work experience, perhaps 40–50 percent of the time.

Many interviewers use an established question sequence for their interviews. This makes a great deal of sense. In this way, the interviewer can monitor his progress and determine if he is about on schedule to gain all the information he needs. Also, the candidate gains the impression that the interview is being conducted in an orderly and systematic fashion. One such interview questions sequence is presented below. It is used by many interviewers and provides a solid framework for gaining the information needed to evaluate a given candidate for a variety of positions.

1. Greeting client and establishing rapport.
2. Overview—explain purpose of meeting; identify general format of discussion; indicate that you will be reviewing some topics already covered in 120 Questionnaire; explain about the company; and indicate the next step in the interviewing process.

3. Early childhood—inquire about incidents, factors, events that influenced later development.

4. Education—high school and college years: best subjects, teachers, activities; college major, interests, accomplishments, jobs, grades, outside activities, current courses, future desired learning.

5. Work experience—each position: activities, bosses, environments liked least and best, promotions, accomplishments, frustrations, conflicts, rewards.

6. Activities—outside job-related interests or activities, travel, relocation, weekend work positions held in professional associations, and so on.

7. Self-description—overall self-description, positions currently best suited for, support required or environments conducive to success, career interests, long-term plans.

8. Supplemental questions—additional questions to be used to identify candidate's specific trait pattern—discussed further in chapter 7.

9. Information on company—provide overview of the organization, the environment, career opportunities, advancement, and so on.

Step 8: Consider Trait-Specific Interview Questions

Material presented in chapter 7 provides the interviewer additional questions to define the candidate further in terms of the seven traits defined in chapter 2. That is, chapter 7 probes some of the subcategories that contribute to the seven basic traits. These questions allow the interviewer, with increasingly specific questions, to understand better the subtraits that further define the seven traits. Questions analyzing topics like planning and organizing, problem analysis, risk taking, judgment, self-esteem, adaptability, and persuasiveness are presented. Also, typical answers from individuals who are representative of the seven types are discussed. These questions may need to be interwoven into the interview at different phases.

5

The Interview Process

Worthwhile interviews, like successful sales presentations, productive meetings, and clever jokes, seem to flow effortlessly. Frequently this result occurs
because the process of the presentation, meeting, or joke has been carefully
controlled. The process of any social interaction is critical to its success. This
chapter reviews some basic information about the process of interviewing
and reminds the interviewer of some basic tools and key ideas to maintain a
smooth, flowing, and productive interview.

The purpose of the interview is to gain valid information about the candidate. This chapter highlights some techniques and ideas to do just that.
Anyone can memorize and ask a series of questions and record the responses; this behavior is not interviewing. The skilled use of proven techniques will facilitate the interview process. This chapter is designed to assist
the interviewer in the information-gathering process of the interview. Generally speaking, the value of these ideas applies to any social interaction, but
especially to interviewing.

The chapter begins with the fundamentals. You must help the applicant
relax before you shift into the real purpose of the interview: obtaining valid
information. This chapter provides benchmark behaviors that develop and
maintain rapport with the candidate and disclose meaningful information
about him. Methods to control the interview as well as to verify information
are presented. Finally, techniques to close the interview effectively are discussed. The ideas are presented in the same sequence as may occur in an
actual interview.

The importance of planning for interviews was addressed in the previous
chapter. Stress was placed on having defined: the requirements of the position, the personal characteristics to be assessed, and the areas of a candidate's background to be explored in detail. These elements may be regarded
as the content of the interview.

It is of equal importance to approach the interview as a process. The word
process is used to denote the dialogue and interchanges that occur between

interviewer and interviewee, and the interviewer uses *process skills* to obtain significant information about the interviewee on which to base conclusions and make decisions. More generally, the skills required for effective interviewing overlap substantially those required for effective interpersonal relationships. In acquiring an understanding of the process objectives of interviewing and the techniques used to achieve them, you will enhance your interviewing skills. The following comments and examples are directed at the employment or selection interview; however, they apply equally well to other categories of interviews.

HELPING THE CANDIDATE RELAX

An employment interview is stressful for most people. It is safe to assume that the major objective of the candidate is to receive a job offer and, therefore, he is interested in making a good impression. That is, he is consciously putting his best foot forward in a deliberate attempt to sell you on the idea of hiring him. He is energized, focused, and probably feeling some level of anxiety about meeting you for the first time. He is slightly tense and eager to start the process.

At the same time, your responsibility is to act in a positive way that also enables you to interview perceptively and evaluate the candidate. In some ways, you may want to act like a recruiter in the sense of projecting a positive image of the company, but at the same time, you are required to evaluate the candidate effectively for a position in the company. You are functioning as both the judge and jury in this situation. This responsibility is serious, and you want to conduct yourself in the best possible fashion.

The result is that the pressure is on you both. The candidate is probably slightly nervous about projecting a valid but positive and upbeat impression. Correspondingly, you are concerned to convey a sense of personal warmth and concern for the candidate as an individual, but you have the additional responsibility to elicit information from him that will help you determine his suitability for employment.

The end result is that both of you are probably a little nervous about the situation. Both of you may be slightly more concerned with your own issues than with the other person. The candidate is primarily interested in selling himself, and the interviewer is primarily interested in questioning the candidate. It is your responsibility, however, to master your own stress and project a polite, rational, and concerned demeanor to the candidate.

This task is not easy. By analogy, have you ever attended a party where you know almost no one? You are walking up to the door, your stomach begins to turn flip-flops, and you feel your stomach acid level rise. You greet the host, and immediately you feel largely at ease and comfortable and generally decide that "this may work out." Afterward, you marvel at the apparently effortless skill of the host in putting people socially at ease and managing a gracious evening. Some people are naturally skilled in such situations, but most people require discipline and practice to acquire the refined grace of the effortless host.

You may be thinking that you possess many technical skills and that you are good at the core elements of your job but that this social polish stuff for the interviewing process is simply not you and you will never be able to "pull it off." So, what is the purpose? It is twofold. First, you can make a significant difference in the interviewing process by learning to be more candidate-oriented, and second, you definitely can improve your interpersonal skills when interviewing.

The famous movie actor Cary Grant, in many of his movies and in real life, was often considered the epitome of social polish and interpersonal skill. As one movie critic put it, "Mr. Grant looks better ruffled than most of us do at ease." When Grant was asked how he came to develop such a refined sense of social interaction, he replied that he just practiced and practiced until he developed into the person that he wanted to be. In much the same way, you can practice being candidate-oriented and focus your energies on making the candidate at ease in your presence.

Some interviewers are seemingly able politely and directly to convey a sincere interest in a candidate. At the same time, these interviewers are also capable of discovering unique strengths and possibly heretofore hidden weaknesses in the same candidate. These interviewers seem to possess X-ray vision that enables them to see through the candidate and to analyze his most private skills and abilities. Some people do possess these skills and can be called naturally gifted interviewers. Most of us, however, have to work at it.

Greeting the Candidate and Establishing Rapport

The first few minutes of an interview are critical for easing the candidate's anxieties and helping him relax. Greeting the candidate in a warm and friendly manner lets him know that you are interested in him and will be easy to talk to. A firm handshake and a friendly smile, delivered while rising and moving forward to greet him by name, convey to the candidate that you consider him deserving of your attention and that he will receive it. In essence, deliberately place your energies on thinking about the candidate and try not to think of yourself. Repress any individual desire to stand out, be noticed, or draw attention to yourself and focus all your energies on the candidate. Deliberately concentrate on making him the most important person in the process. Try to recall the feeling of joy and acceptance you felt when arriving at that party where everyone was a stranger and where the host immediately made you feel both welcome and comfortable.

The successful completion of this initial part of the interview will accomplish two important items:

1. It establishes that the company (in the person of you) cares about the candidates and, presumably by extension, that the company cares about the people that work here. This message is important whether the candidate is offered a position or not. That is, in general, you want candidates to have a positive impression of the company.
2. Establishing this initial feeling of goodwill and comfort will enable the candidate to relax and be more himself. The candidate is then more inclined to let his real self come through, and your job of investigating the candidate is much easier. That is, he will be less defensive or anxious and is more likely to express candidly his true strengths and weaknesses.

In most instances, the candidate will assume that you will establish the direction of the interview, especially at the beginning. Oftentimes, the first opportunity you have to exercise this influence will be the seating arrangements. Accordingly, indicating where you wish the candidate to sit is sometimes helpful. Some research suggests that the candidate will feel more comfortable if both of you are sitting on a couch or at a table away from your desk. In general, avoid, if possible, seating arrangements that create a feeling of formality or distance. A desk that separates you from a candidate is sometimes perceived as a barrier to open communication and thus reduces your efforts to create an atmosphere of comfort and mutual trust.

At the same time, however, it is important that you feel comfortable in the seating arrangements. If you are not comfortable sitting on a couch with the candidate, if you feel more at ease near your desk, and, perhaps most important, if you project a greater comfort being near your desk, then use your desk in the interviewing process. If you do use the desk, however, you should probably arrange for the candidate to sit at the side of the desk and for you to sit behind the desk. In this way, you can sit at right angles to each other. Numerous research studies point out that improved communication occurs when people sit at right angles to each other, rather than in any other arrangement.

Be conscious of your own feelings and what your body language may be communicating. Polite attentiveness is behaviorally different from outright tenseness. Obvious anxiety on your part or an overly formal or direct approach will increase rather than decrease the candidate's own stress. Take a second to review your own Personal Analysis Chart as defined in the last chapter and reflect if your own behavior style will have an unintended effect on the candidate.

For example, the overachiever sometimes tends to sit ramrod straight in the chair and ask questions in a manner indicative of an inquisition more than a polite conversation. This person maintains a constant and steady gaze at the candidate that may be his way of naturally interacting. The overachiever may conduct the interview in a very rational and logical manner and follow all the recommended steps in exact order, but he can unintentionally convey a sense of mechanical routine.

The entrepreneur can be a potentially overpowering interviewer because he appears to be so self-confident and polished that he comes across in a slightly conceited way. This person can impress others as being so self-concerned that he has little time, emotion, or energy to share with the candidate. The entrepreneur, however, is generally quite perceptive at reading the candidate. He is able to understand intuitively, evaluate, and critically appraise the candidate quickly and accurately.

The active person can have just the opposite effect. The high active likes everybody and is eager to share his own life experiences with the candidate. The active is truly likable and generally thinks everyone else is too. Unfortunately, the active person forgets that he is assigned the responsibility to interview the candidate and not merely share mutual life experiences with him. That is, the active may have to guard against talking too much about himself and not asking the candidate about himself.

The passive interviewer can project the image of being cautious, methodical, and precise, but also unenthusiastic and pedestrian. At the same time, he will probably communicate a good deal of empathy and concern for the candidate, but he needs to be aware of his tendency to move at a slow pace and his possible inherent desire to avoid making a mistake in hiring someone. Hence, many passive interviewers indicate that "although some of the candidates look reasonable, no one is really outstanding." The passive interviewer is generally in favor of interviewing more candidates and is slow to recommend any one candidate.

The sensitized person can have an effect on candidates totally different from that of the active. The natural social shyness of the sensitized person may cause him to have difficulty asking wholly appropriate questions of a candidate. The result can be that the sensitized person may appear uninterested in the candidate when actually just the opposite is true. The sensitized is frequently highly interested in a candidate, but in a clinical or diagnostic way. Generally, the sensitized person is the most perceptive of all the behavior types and will have the most valid insights into a given candidate; however, he may have difficulty communicating them because he dislikes the idea of being too judgmental about others.

The aggressive person can be overpowering and impressive without being unduly intimidating. The aggressive person who is truly comfortable with himself frequently possesses a sense of social power, control, and influence. He is an impressive person, and he knows it. His manner, bearing, and overall behavior suggest a comfort with positions of power and influence. This person can be most effective by deliberately downplaying his own sense of control. By demonstrating to the candidate some modesty and polite casualness, the aggressive person will convey a sense of acceptance and camaraderie with the candidate. This attitude will enable the candidate to relax during the interview and to tell his own story. The less secure aggressive person may come to an interview with bulging muscles, in a short-sleeve shirt, with crew-cut hair, and with introductory remarks about the need to raise the productivity of the average American worker.

Any interviewer with a predominance of the traits mentioned above can cause problems for two reasons. First, the interviewer may be sending signals that he is uncomfortable in this role; that is, he can be perceived as being more interested in himself and not especially interested in the candidate. Second, the interviewer may be telegraphing to the candidate the kind of behavior that he expects in people who want to work for the company.

Invest a few minutes in making casual conversation and choose a topic of interest to the candidate from the clues provided in the application blank and/or the 120 Questionnaire. For example, if the candidate's 120 Questionnaire mentioned an interest in sports and a significant sporting event recently took place, you can say something like, "I noticed that you were captain of your football team in high school and played some ball in college. Did you see the X game last weekend?" This simple statement quickly conveys three thoughts to the candidate: (1) you read his 120 Questionnaire (and probably other material as well) fairly carefully, (2) you have an interest in him as a person, and (3) you have at least one mutual interest—football and perhaps sports in general. This approach will improve the likelihood that the candidate will relax more and share his real self with you.

Communicate to the candidate, through verbal and nonverbal means, that you are listening closely to what he is saying. For instance, make comments or ask questions that build upon his previous statement or reply. Avoid interrupting him or shifting from topic to topic. Body language, such as a smile, a nod, leaning forward, and so on, also conveys interest. Eye contact is an especially forceful means of communication. It is surprisingly easy to control the flow and content of a conversation with people by the effective use of eye contact.

Numerous studies have highlighted this point. For example, one frequently cited study demonstrated how a group of college students influenced a college professor to stand in one particular place while giving an entire lecture. Their methods were ingeniously well organized and simple. Whenever the professor moved to the right half of the room, the students looked interested in his presentation, were apparently motivated to listen intently, and began to take lengthy notes. Whenever the professor moved to the left half of the room, the same students would begin to yawn, look around the room, and generally demonstrate bored behavior. Eventually the students were able to influence the professor to stand in one particular place and simply shift his weight back and forth from one foot to the other without stepping away. This result was accomplished without the students' saying one word; the professor's behavior was influenced entirely by eye contact. Additional research studies have pointed out that if used in moderation, eye contact can be extremely effective in interviewing; however, it can also be highly intimidating if used excessively.

Organizing the Interview

The candidate obviously knows the objective of an employment interview. Nevertheless, he will likely be anxious about the direction of this particular interview and what will be expected of him in it. He probably has expectations and preconceptions based on past experiences with a variety of interview methods. Therefore, a brief comment at the beginning as to why you are interviewing the candidate and what you hope to accomplish will be helpful in establishing a structure.

The unknown and the unexpected make many people uncomfortable. Addressing this issue by furnishing a general map of the course you intend to follow and the content areas you intend to explore during the interview will ease this anxiety. For example, you might say, "We'll need to review your general background, education, work history, appropriate interests, etc. I'm particularly interested in learning what you're looking for in a job." Simply ask, "OK?" Most candidates will respond with some affirmative answer. Then you should say something like, "I can appreciate that you may have some questions about us [the company] too, but I would like to hold off discussing any of those topics until the end of the interview. OK?" Again, the candidate will respond with a positive answer.

Finally, you should probably set an approximate time frame for conducting the interview by saying something like, "My interviews usually last between 30 and 60 minutes. Sometimes they seem to go more quickly; sometimes they take a little longer. Is that a reasonable period of time for us?" Again, the candidate will be positive.

These three questions accomplish more important parameters of the interview process. By phrasing your comments as rhetorical questions, you are limiting the possible answers, but you are also deliberately including the candidate in the interview process. You are, in a sense, asking for his consent to proceed in the prescribed manner. You are taking the next step to make him feel comfortable in the process.

The first question provides the candidate with a simple outline of the topics you want to cover, and so he generally knows what to expect. The second question requests him to hold off his questions until you are finished asking him about himself; in this way you will not inadvertently tell him your most important criteria for filling a job. Naturally you want to discuss, in some format, the job requirements, but you will tell him at your pace so you can determine his real strengths and not just hear his attempts to tell you what he thinks you may want to hear. Third, you provide him a time frame for the whole interview. In the event that the candidate is clearly not qualified for the position, you can end the process politely but quickly at the end of 30 minutes.

In general, follow the rule of common sense; that is, recognize that the interview is a dialogue between two people. You have things to accomplish, and so does the candidate. Let him know that you will keep his needs in mind. Either ask him directly what he wishes to accomplish or tell him you will make certain to reserve time for answering his questions.

If the candidate insists on obtaining job information first, you should probably answer questions about the job. Limit your remarks, however, to defining the duties and responsibilities required. Avoid describing the type of person you are seeking. A perceptive candidate may use this information to twist his answers to fit your description. It is also wise at this time to avoid a general discussion of the company and selling the job. These topics are best left until such time as you decide this candidate is worth pursuing.

OBTAINING INFORMATION

The main purpose of the interview is to secure information with which you can make an informed decision. After you have engaged the candidate in comfortable conversation and let him know the purposes and general structure of the interview, it is time to guide the interview in the direction of encouraging him to disclose himself and his experiences.

Comprehensive Introductory and Open-ended Questions

Questions that are designed to be somewhat broad and nonspecific are extremely useful for more than one reason. They permit the candidate to choose how he wishes to respond and allow him the leeway to display his original thinking. Also, they generate a less static and more conversational flavor in the interview. In bringing about the move from rapport building to information gathering, a comprehensive introductory question is more useful.

As an example, you might say, "I would like to cover four general areas with you today: (1) your early childhood experiences and education; (2) your work experiences, starting with your first full-time job and culminating with your most recent employment; (3) some discussion of how you see yourself, your strengths and weaknesses, and how you might handle particular situations; and (4) then, as I said earlier, I will provide you some information on the company. Now, that is a lot of territory to cover so let's take it one area at a time, OK?"

Once the candidate agrees to the outline you have proposed, you should continue with a statement like, "Starting with the first area, please tell me about your early childhood from about age seven on—where you went to school, your neighborhood, your activities in grade school and high school, where you went to college, your school major, academic performance, rea-

Northland College
Dexter Library
Ashland, WI 54806

sons for choosing that college, how these experiences prepared you for adult life in general, and, more especially, how the experiences prepared you for the duties of this position."

Why begin the interview with a review of the candidate's early life? This is something that the candidate should know fairly well and (if you have established some level of rapport with him) that he should be willing to discuss. It provides an easy transition point and also gives you some of the most important information for understanding the development of his behavior style. Chapter 3 provides many examples and clues for interpreting the candidate's responses to this part of the interview.

For the balance of the interview, open-ended questions should be used as much as possible. An open-ended question places few limits on the candidate and requires an interpretive response, for example, "Why did you attend State University?" In contrast a closed-ended question can be answered in one or two words, for example, "Why did you attend State University from 1971 to 1975?" More examples of an open-ended question are: "Tell me about your development during your high schools years" and "What are some of the aspects of your current position that you especially like or dislike?"

As a rule, open-ended questions are among the most effective during the interview process and should be used throughout it. Properly used, they invite/require the candidate to open up and discuss himself. By their very nature, these questions require him to focus his thoughts and discuss topics that are important to him.

Remember, however, that these kinds of questions are difficult for some people to deal with. If you sense the candidate is being made anxious by the questions, move to more direct questioning for a period and resume the open-ended questions at a fitting time. Examples of more direct questions are: "Did you enjoy your college years?" and "Would Saturday meetings be a problem for you?"

Generally speaking, these direct questions can be answered with a simple yes, no, or another very short answer. They also allow you to ask additional, follow-up questions, such as, "Can you help me understand in more detail some of the particular things you liked about college?" Direct questions can be useful in dealing with people who tend to wander in their answers. For example, some candidates initially take responsibility for a vast array of job functions but, when more directly questioned, tone down their accomplishments. Also, some lower-level personnel feel more comfortable answering more direct questions; they can be overwhelmed by open-ended questions and need the implied structure of more direct questioning.

Use of Reinforcement

It is important that the rapport you established initially be sustained throughout the interview. As stated earlier, candidates are usually anxious to please and to have a favorable impact on the interviewer. If you keep this fact in mind, reinforcement of the candidate's behavior can be used to sustain rapport. Reinforcement can be thought of as a rewarding behavior (verbal or nonverbal) that induces the candidate to persist with what he is doing. For instance, paying close attention to what the candidate is saying is a reinforcing behavior. In fact, the attending behaviors used in establishing rapport should be used throughout the interview.

Remember, how you behave will significantly affect the behavior of the candidate. A relatively unexpressive style, deliberate in its attempt to provide minimal feedback, is used by some interviewers. Frequently these interviewers see this technique as a way of applying some mild pressure on the candidate. These interviewers then feel they can gain a better evaluation of the candidate and his ability to react to sudden or unexpected pressure. This technique does induce some anxiety in most candidates, and their responses are not a valid barometer of their ability to handle stress.

The unfortunate response of many candidates to this type of interviewing is often an assumption that the unresponsiveness indicates a negative reaction. The candidate then begins to change his responses and tries to get a more positive reaction from the interviewer. For example, he may start to talk more quickly, giving more information to which the interviewer can react, or he may use more dramatic, exaggerated, or otherwise emotionally loaded words or statements. Additionally, he may begin to rephrase and/or repeat himself, assuming that his first attempts had little or no impact.

This pattern of deliberate silence on the part of the interviewer and the patterned responses it elicits from the candidate are both predictable and typical. Even the most experienced (in the sense of being interviewed) candidates will exhibit these behaviors.

This approach serves no useful purpose. The candidate is responding in a manner that is atypical of him but very predictable from the situation, and he is probably interpreting the interview as a negative experience. So, if he is selected for the position, he may carry negative feelings for the person who interviewed him for some time. Conversely, if he is not selected for the position, he may well feel negatively toward the interviewer and the company.

Elaboration Techniques

In the ideal world every candidate would respond with thorough, detailed, and well-organized answers to every question. In the real world of interviewing, this situation does not happen. It is essential, therefore, to have at your disposal the skills and techniques for gracefully extracting additional information from a candidate.

You should not be hesitant about asking specific questions about a candidate's response so that you can clarify a point or get added information.

Especially important is exploring the reasoning behind the candidate's past decisions and his perspectives on his experiences. Questions like "Why did you do such-and-such?" and "How did you feel about that?" should come automatically to you. Simply asking the candidate to elaborate (e.g., "Please tell me more about that") frequently results in more details being supplied.

There are other, less obvious, and less direct methods that can be used to encourage the candidate to provide more depth or elaboration to a response. A single word or even an encouraging nonverbal reaction, delivered after a candidate's response, can effectively induce him to speak further (e.g., an understanding nod of the head or an interested "Oh?").

Another method you may find useful is to repeat inquiringly one or two words used by a candidate in his response. For example, a candidate might state that he liked the variety provided in his previous job. You might simply say, "Variety?" This approach will extract more information and, additionally, allow you, by the words you choose to repeat, to direct the interview toward the areas that particularly interest you.

The last technique to be considered in this section is the use of silence or a pause. Periods of silence in an interview raise considerable anxiety in most inexperienced interviewers and even in many veterans. Remind yourself that many of the questions you ask will and should require some thought to be answered. The human brain cannot, like a computer, respond in microseconds. Questions that are complex and that kindle thinking require consideration and time to be answered. The more complex and more thought-provoking the question, the more time needed to answer it.

In addition, the judicious use of pauses after a candidate responds can be a compelling means of extracting further information. It is, in some respects, a specialized way of reinforcing. If used moderately, the pause provides a contrast to your behavior throughout most of the interview, during which you have been responding with comments and questions that reflect the fact that you have been listening carefully to what he has been saying. Because of the difference, the candidate will be more likely to notice a pause on your part and react to it. You are communicating, in effect: "Tell me more. What you've said is not exactly what I was looking for."

DIRECTING AND CONTROLLING THE INTERVIEW

As most interviews are scheduled for a limited time period, one of your responsibilities as an interviewer will be to make efficient use of the time. You will need to estimate the amount of time needed, based on your experience in interviewing candidates at a given level. At best, this estimate will be rough. Many variable factors, such as the extent of work experience, length of answers, expansiveness of the candidate, and so on, will affect how long an interview will run. This section will present techniques that will help in planning for the use of interview time.

A smooth flow of conversation from area to area is desirable. Therefore, the ideal interview plan should include an outline of a logical progression for you to follow. It is unlikely that the candidate will follow your outline exactly, despite your attempts, so you must be flexible. You must be prepared to provide subtle urging and guidance, with occasional directness and assertiveness, to lead the candidate in the directions you wish to pursue. But you must also follow his agenda when it, for the moment, diverges from your own.

The previous section illustrated several techniques useful in encouraging elaboration by the candidate. This section discusses how active, selective listening can be used to extract a wider variety of information and guide the direction of the interview.

Moving through the Various Background Areas

Picking up on cues provided by a candidate's responses may be the easiest and least controlling way to direct an interview. In effect, you can take advantage of openings the candidate provides for you. As an example, imagine an interview in which you have covered the candidate's work history for perhaps 15 or 20 minutes and want to move on. The candidate has just mentioned, in reference to his current position, how understaffed his department is and how frequently he has to travel. This statement could provide you with the opening for a leading comment, such as "That must cut down on your leisure time," followed by a more open-ended question: "What kind of activities do you like to pursue in your leisure time?" Obviously, to use this approach effectively, you must listen carefully and attentively.

In instances where the candidate does not provide such cues or a time limit does not allow waiting for one, you should introduce a transition question. Here are examples of transition questions: "I can see you crammed a great deal into your four years at college. Now, give me some feel for your work history. Let's start with your first 'real' job and work up to the present" and "You have been very thorough in describing your work experiences. Please help me understand how you spend some of your leisure time."

In this way you will communicate more directly that you wish to move on to a new area, but the transition will be less abrupt than if you simply asked a question unrelated to the present topic.

Focusing on Facts or Feelings

In assessing the individual, you will need factual data. Certain information, such as what school he attended and how he did there and where he last worked and what his responsibilities were, is essential for you to know. Also, to understand him better, you will want to know why he chose to do certain things at certain times.

One equally important source of information is, however, often overlooked by many inexperienced interviewers: the feelings the person has about his experiences and about himself. A distinction is made by psychologists between the thinking (cognitive) level and the feeling (affective) level.

Appropriately phrasing your questions is one way to direct the interview toward either the cognitive or the affective area. In general, questions that ask for specific factual information (e.g., "What were your duties on that job?") or that inquire into a person's reasoning (e.g., "Why didn't you accept that promotion?") will elicit cognitive responses. On the other hand, questions that probe the emotional aspect of an experience (e.g., "How do you feel about the time you spent at Acme?") will direct the candidate toward the affective level. More open-ended questions allow the candidate more latitude in choosing the level from which he responds.

You may have some difficulty in getting the candidate to concentrate on the affective level. In our business-oriented culture, thinking is often valued over feeling. The candidate is a product of that culture, and he is also trying to make a good impression. Also, remember that you are still a comparative stranger to him, despite the rapport you have worked to establish.

There is another technique (one that builds on the candidate's responses) that can be used, in addition to specific questioning, to direct the interview toward either the thinking or the feeling level. The technique is called selective listening.

In selective listening, all or part of a candidate's response is rephrased. Restating the basic content (idea) of a response is termed paraphrasing. If the restatement embodies the emotional tone of the response, it is termed reflection. An example will help you understand this distinction.

Interviewer: Why would you consider leaving your present company?

Candidate: Well, it may sound conceited, but I have reached my sales goals, and they put a cap on my earnings. That doesn't seem fair to me.

Interviewer:

Paraphrase: So they are effectively limiting your income.

Reflection: I get the impression you feel frustrated with the compensation formula.

Notice the paraphrasing and reflecting are actually a more extensive or elaborate variant of minimal cues. Minimal cues should not be overlooked as techniques for directing or controlling the interview.

VERIFYING INFORMATION AND CLARIFYING CONFUSION

There will be times when there appear to be inconsistencies or even contradictions in a candidate's responses, however honest and communicative he may be. Do not assume that these apparent discrepancies are deliberate. One of the most consistent characteristics of human nature is its amazing inconsistency at times. One of your jobs, as an interviewer, is to determine which are real (actual) inconsistencies and which are apparent inconsistencies, arising from inadequate communication.

Another potential origin of confusion is the communication skill of the candidate. Of course, the effectiveness of your own listening skills will affect how clearly you understand what he says, but, no matter how skillful you are, occasionally you will be struck with a sense that you are not completely certain that you understand what was said. In this section, we will investigate ways of handling this kind of situation.

Handling Contradictions and Inconsistencies

Inconsistencies are presented by most people in at least some of their behaviors. A way of dealing with them is to expand the scope and amount of information you have about the candidate. Consider, for example, a situation where it seems the candidate was impulsive and emotional in choosing one job but extremely cautious and analytical in choosing another. In such a case, it is advisable to explore other instances where he made key decisions so that you can establish his most typical decision-making behavior.

Second, on occasion, you might approach the problem directly by stating your confusion or calling attention to apparent inconsistencies. This technique can be quite effective. It should be used sparingly and with prudence, however, since a poorly phrased or timed comment can quickly ruin the feeling of openness and trust you have worked to achieve. Avoid implying that you do not believe the candidate. Rather, let him know you are having trouble resolving what seem to be some disparities in his responses and need his assistance in doing so.

A third way of checking and clarifying information is to use summary statements. The earlier discussion of selective listening introduced the concepts of paraphrase and reflection, which are brief, modified restatements of the responses of the candidate. A summary statement is also a restatement but is broader and more extensive and encompasses, in an organizing way, information given in more than one candidate response over a longer period during the interview.

In an employment interview, most summary statements are directed at the content and factual information contained in a candidate's responses. Consequently, they are referred to as summary paraphrases. Other types of interviews (e.g., counseling, disciplinary, and so on) are more likely to include summary reflections.

Focusing to Clarify Confusion

The preceding section dealt primarily with inconsistencies and confusion that arise from a rather wide range of responses. You will undoubtedly also confront instances where you experience confusion after one specific response from the candidate.

You might deal directly with such an instance by simply asking for further explanation (e.g., you might state, "I'm not certain I follow what you are saying"). The other elaboration techniques mentioned earlier in this section, such as using minimal cues, silence, or selective listening, could also be used. A paraphrase, preceded perhaps by an introductory "What I hear is . . . ," will almost certainly induce the candidate to clarify what he said.

CONCLUDING THE INTERVIEW

A discussion of some objectives and techniques that can be used in generating a comfortable climate for the interview began this chapter. It is appropriate now to end with a discussion of several points that you need to consider as you wind down and ultimately conclude the interview.

Answering Candidate's Questions

Most job candidates have certain questions they want answered by the interviewer. As you gain more experience, you will cultivate a feeling for the type of information for which a candidate typically looks. Generally, it is best to be as thorough and candid as possible. Considering time limitations, however, if you feel the candidate is obviously unqualified, you may choose to provide less than complete information.

Ultimately, the final decision as to whether a candidate you are interested in hiring will join your organization is his. You must, at the very minimum, give him the information he feels he needs to make a decision. If you do not have the information he requests, let him know you will get it and relay it to him.

The significance of your personal impact should not be disregarded as a factor that will influence the candidate in making a decision. Most likely, you are the one person in the organization with whom he has been most involved. Just as you have evaluated him on the evidence of what he has said and his behavior, he will evaluate you. He will be influenced in making his decision by, among other things, the degree of knowledge you have of the company and of the job under consideration, your enthusiasm and confidence, and your skill in relating to him.

There are few general principles or specific techniques to aid you here. Specific guidelines are provided by some organizations as to what information they do and do not want communicated to a candidate. Beyond this guide, your personal preference is often the only basis for proceeding. Under these circumstances, probably it is best to use the approach you find most comfortable.

Structuring the Closing

Usually, it will be clear to the candidate that the interview is nearing completion. We suggest that part of your regular practice include inviting the

candidate to bring up any topic of importance to him that was not covered
and to ask any questions he might have. If you are definitely interested in a
candidate, take care to define clearly and specifically the next step(s) taken
in the hiring procedure. Usually, it is judicious to postpone a decision until
you have taken the time to review your notes and to compare your impressions with others who have dealt with the candidate, even if you hold the
authority to make the decision.

We do not suggest that you avoid giving any feedback to the candidate.
There is no point in the interview when his need for feedback is likely to be
greater. Only the more assertive candidates will ask directly about the likelihood of their being offered a position, but all, no doubt, will wonder. If you
definitely want to hire a candidate or even if you just consider him still a
possibility, it is generally sufficient to tell him that he appears to fit the job
well but that you must interview all candidates before a decision can be
made.

Many interviewers choose to use the same tactic with candidates they will
ultimately reject. Something can be said for this approach. If you have a
fixed time limit, it may just take too long to spend even a few minutes on
giving feedback to the candidate. There is the risk, unless you are completely
familiar with the legal facets of hiring procedures, that inadvertently and
with the best of motives, you may give him grounds for a lawsuit. In the case
of a candidate with whom you feel you have good rapport and who is well
motivated and non-defensive, you may wish to give him some specific feedback or information that will be helpful to him.

THE INTERVIEW PROCESS AND THE SEVEN TYPES

We have covered a long list of interview process topics in this chapter.
Now let's integrate some of these process information techniques with specific examples of candidates representing the seven behavior types.

Each of the types can present special opportunities or difficulties for the
interviewer, and the sooner you are aware of the candidate's probable behavior style, the better you can adapt yourself to the interview process and gain
meaningful information from the interview itself.

The key to the process is to remember that most candidates will be slightly
nervous for the interview and will be consciously and deliberately trying to
project their best image. Generally this intention means that they will more
readily demonstrate their natural behavior style. Remember that everyone's
behavior generally makes sense, at least to him. For example, the active
person will be more energized and outgoing. The sensitized may be initially
more shy and therefore require more time to establish that important sense
of rapport and mutual trust.

In terms of obtaining information from the overachiever, he can initially
appear slightly formal and emotionally reticent, but he is highly organized

and will appreciate any steps you take to be equally organized. He will respond to straightforward questions and will answer them in a methodical and factual manner. He may or may not respond to your attempts at social warmth and may see attempts at specific reinforcement as unnecessary; after all, he thinks the facts are obvious.

He will, however, recognize and appreciate your asking questions in a matter-of-fact fashion. He is proud of his accomplishments, and although not inclined to embellish them, he will state them in a deliberate manner. For example, he may say, "I completed college while working part-time and then started my first job." When asked for more details, he may then include that he also graduated with honors, was involved in a social service organization, and worked a full-time swing shift his senior year.

He has no problem switching his attention from one area of his background to another. He may be quite pleased to do this switching because it will enable him subtly to relay how he demonstrated his sense of self-discipline in another area of his life. He does tend to focus on the facts of the situation and may resent any suggestion that he should divulge his emotional attitudes during an interview. As a rule, the overachiever prides himself on explaining his material quite carefully. If, however, something is unclear in his history, he will repeat it without showing any embarrassment or hesitation. For him, falsehoods are too difficult to remember, and so lying about his record is not on his agenda.

He may have some questions about the mechanical aspects of the position or company policies in a given area. He may ask about long-term development in the company and truly be interested in the possibility of developing a career with the company. He tends to commit himself to long-term projects that will have a productive end.

The entrepreneur is generally ready and eager to share positive information about himself but may be inclined to shade or glance over facts that reflect less well on himself; he is not so much being devious as he is merely being true to his own behavior style. He likes to accentuate the positive aspects of his accomplishments and tends to see his failures as the result of another person's mistakes. He may respond to an open-ended question with a question of his own, like: "That's a pretty broad question. What exactly do you mean?" Typically this response means that he is less interested in answering your question and candidly telling you about himself than he is in gaining some insight into what he thinks you want to hear.

The entrepreneur is very clever at distilling any available clues about what you are looking for in a candidate and will carefully attempt to portray himself in that light. At the same time, he is a competitive person and will respond to any hint of reinforcement. If, for example, you indicate an interest in a given area, he will readily talk at length about his accomplishments during a given time frame.

The entrepreneur will generally appear willing to discuss any aspect of his background that you feel is important. If, however, he appears to want to jump over a given topic, he may be hiding something. For example, he may imply that he completed college, but when probed, he will admit that he completed a junior college degree, that he has since finished several industry courses in X, and that this combination is (in his opinion, anyway) the equivalent of a college degree. Despite your own judgments about his manner of explaining his actions this way, you may be wise to suggest that you agree with his conclusion. In this way, if he thinks that you agree with his perspective, he will be more inclined to tell you other incidents that may reflect on his perception of other factors in his background. For example, he may indicate that (contrary to the information on the 120 Questionnaire) he did not really qualify for every sales convention, but for most of them.

In a similar vein you should not be too surprised to catch the entrepreneur in some inconsistencies in his verbal presentation. Again, however, do not overemphasize the point with him but politely clarify any confusion and suggest that you misunderstood him the first time. If he feels that you are increasingly aware of his stretching some facts, he will be more selective in what he tells you. Remember, to see the candidate as he actually is, you must provide him an atmosphere to be comfortable with you. Afterward, when you are reviewing all your notes, you can more easily decide if a given candidate inflated his accomplishments beyond the reasonable limits of what your company will accept.

The active person is happy to share honestly information about himself with almost anybody. He may gladly volunteer more information than you may be comfortable hearing. Remember, the active is a team person and generally thinks everyone should share and partake of any information he wants. He is not ashamed or afraid of admitting too much and will candidly describe his failures and successes with little prompting. He likes to talk, and if you are willing to listen, he will typically give you an earful. Moreover, he can ramble in response to some open-ended questions, and it may be necessary to use some direct questioning to control his responses.

The active person is pleased to switch from one topic area to another. Variety in all its forms is the spice of his life. He will happily discuss growing up, his work experiences, and his current leisure activities. Personal feelings about a given topic are equally available from the active. You may incorrectly interpret him as being too sensitive based exclusively on his verbal responses to cues about how he feels about certain situations. The active will readily state that he has been frustrated, happy, and at times emotionally down; however, his willingness to admit to these emotions is also evidence for the fact that they quickly pass.

As a rule, the active is an honest and reliable person. He can, however, be confused about details and may appear to contradict himself. He is probably not deliberately hiding anything, but he may simply have too much on his mind and be overly eager to share his ideas with you. Generally, he will respond to a comment that he is going too fast and that you need him simply to slow down and explain his activities more carefully. His company-related questions may focus on the people in the company. He wants to know what kind of social atmosphere exists in the organization and whether his style will fit in.

The passive candidate can be slow to respond to questions, although, when politely pressed, he too will respond in a factual manner. His appearance may be slightly defensive, or his delivery may be a little slow and drawn-out, but he will tell a complete story. It is necessary to go slowly with this person and allow him to relate his story at a comfortable pace. He will switch from one area to another but may want specific instructions to do so. Some passive candidates will mention feelings of unsureness, tension, or a need for structure in their employment. Also, they can be somewhat negative and may mention a crummy work environment to describe their former employers.

Moreover, feelings of frustration and the fact they were upset by some work-related act for a period of time suggest a passive. You may be confused or frustrated listening to the passives' history, but they generally will not contradict themselves. They move at a slow but steady pace, and although they seldom reach significant production goals without prodding, they equally seldom make mistakes in their record keeping. So, the passive's presentation will be methodical, slow, and somewhat plodding but not offensive, and it seldom has contradictions or even accidental errors.

The sensitized candidate can be the most ill at ease about providing information about himself. He is a private and shy person. Information that the active person might readily tell anyone, the sensitized can have difficulty telling close friends. The rapport-building stage is especially important with him. Once he feels comfortable with you, he will be more inclined to provide you more significant details of his life; however, this presentation can take extra time. Your personal sincerity and credibility are especially important to the sensitized candidate. He is probably more comfortable responding to technical questions about his work than revealing his feelings about a given topic.

In handling apparent contradictions with the sensitized person, remember that he is sensitive in general and especially about issues of personal propriety. He would resent the implication that he had misstated something. You certainly have the right and obligation to double-check what may be an error in dates, timing, or history, but be sure to do so with care and due respect for his feelings. Finally, this candidate may need to be prodded to ask questions about the firm. He may have them but be too anxious or shy to ask them. Once reassured that asking questions is allowed, he can be expected to ask insightful and meaningful questions.

The aggressive type can also be sensitive about some questions but will try to deny his "thin-skinness" and may consciously try to control the interview.

The entrepreneur may tend to exaggerate his monetary accomplishments, especially in terms of how much product he sold, while the aggressive person may expand his record in terms of the authority, responsibility, and control he exercised. He may remember his role as being slightly enlarged compared to his actual duties. He sees himself as a person who should (if he does not necessarily already) hold a position of control and influence in his group, so he is likely to "fluff up" this area during the interview.

He has little difficulty changing topics during the interview and can see each new topic as an opportunity to talk politely about his accomplishments in a given area. The aggressive person wants to take control of most situations, and he is likely to see new topics as vehicles to express his success in a variety of situations. He is slow to talk about his feelings but generally will allow he experienced some frustration, but primarily as a vehicle to take greater responsibility in his next position.

The aggressive candidate can be quite sensitive about having his authority questioned, and he is likely to interpret any suggestion that his statements are inconsistent or confusing as a threat to his authority. So it is necessary to circumvent these issues and ask about them indirectly or to pretend ignorance on your part. The aggressive enjoys teaching, proclaiming, and announcing; hence, the opportunity to help you better understand the nature of his accomplishments may be well received. His interview-ending questions will likely focus on advancement opportunities and a request for a discussion of his possible career path. He typically wants to know who is on first and what is the fastest route to get ahead.

CONCLUSION

A word of caution: there is a danger, as with any book dealing with techniques, that specific techniques may be used mechanically, without consideration of the user's individual style and the distinctive characteristics and variety of the people with whom he will be dealing. Even though a technique may, in general, be extremely useful, if it does not fit your particular style or if you are uncomfortable using it, it will be ineffective. Nor will the technique accomplish what you intend if it is not used with the appropriate timing. Our closing advice is to rehearse and experiment with these techniques over a fair amount of time and modify them to fit your style.

6

Interpreting the 220 Questionnaire

Appendix B includes a blank 220 Questionnaire. This questionnaire lists a number of possible topic areas and corresponding questions to be reviewed during the interview. The questions were arranged around a set number of topics. The purpose of asking these specific questions is to compare the candidate's responses to the questions with the responses from individuals with known levels of interpersonal skill and behavior styles. These comparisons allow us to define, measure, and interpret the candidate's responses in such a way that the interviewer gains additional insight into the candidate's behavior style. This chapter provides an analysis of those questions. Reading it should enable you to feel increasingly self-confident about your ability to interview a given candidate perceptively. Moreover, you should feel comfortable defining his behavior style and rating his level of interpersonal skill on a series of dimensions.

The section numbers and the question topics listed in appendix B are directly related to the information contained in this chapter. The final two sections of the 220 Questionnaire—information on the company and the conclusion—are covered by the interviewer, and comments are found in appendix B. Just as appendix B is more than a collection of questions to be asked in an interview, this chapter is more than a collection of typical answers given by the different behavior types. The material in these two parts is presented somewhat mechanically so that you can review the ideas contained in the parts in an organized and sequential fashion. The purpose of these parts is to assist you to refine and enhance your interviewing skills. Specifically, these two parts focus on identifying the candidate's interpersonal strengths and potential weaknesses as you evaluate them in the interview.

The purpose of this book is to improve your assessment of interpersonal skills in the interview. The seven behavior traits defined in the first chapter are the cornerstone of that understanding. Individuals can be defined by rating them high, medium, or low on those seven traits, but a more explicit definition of a candidate is also possible. This chapter is designed to give you the information (when used with the information gained by reviewing the 120 Questionnaire responses) that will enable you to define a candidate's interpersonal skills more carefully.

The chapter's focus is on the candidate's responses to the questions and how to interpret them to understand better the candidate's interpersonal strengths and weaknesses. The responses to Parts 1, 2, and 4 of the 220 Questionnaire are analyzed solely in terms of the seven traits introduced in the first chapter. The responses to Part 3 of the 220 Questionnaire are analyzed in terms of these same seven traits and the additional temperament traits that are listed in Part 3 of the 220 Questionnaire.

PART 1: INTRODUCTION

Establish Rapport

You have already reviewed the 120 Questionnaire, so you should have some idea about the candidate's background, education, and work history. You may wish to comment about some information he has indicated in the 120 Questionnaire and demonstrate that you are generally familiar with his background. For example, you may comment and ask about some activity, sport, college major, or work experience that you had in common with him to increase the degree of rapport between you. This is important because you want the candidate to relax and be himself. Naturally there is some degree of stress involved in the interview process, but, generally, the more relaxed the candidate, the easier he is to understand.

The overachiever candidate may have some difficulty showing a relaxed mood. He is by definition a self-controlled and disciplined person. This description does not mean that he is socially inflexible, but it suggests that he can be more formal than other candidates. His appearance is simple, neat, and unaffected. As a rule he will prefer white shirts, lace-up shoes, and dark, businesslike clothing. He may appear somewhat emotionally stiff at first, but he is alert and responsive to any cues you provide him about beginning the task of the interview.

The entrepreneur candidate may show a moment of formality and stiffness—while he attempts to understand you and thereby modify his approach to suit what he perceives to be your needs. The entrepreneur is highly perceptive in reading people and very quick to modify his own approach to fit his expectations of what his audience wants to see. As a rule, however, he thinks that slick appearance, smooth demeanor, and polished social presence are appropriate for almost any occasion. He leans toward razor-cut hair, monogrammed shirts, and French cuffs. He is socially polished and apparently highly self-confident. He will readily respond to your attempts at rapport building and may in turn ask about your experiences that may match his—he is interested in building a sense of rapport too.

The active candidate may be standing in the waiting room when you arrive to meet him. He is typically energetic and has a difficult time sitting still. The active person likes color in his dress and may be wearing colorful but appropriate clothing. The active candidate readily responds to efforts toward rapport building. He instinctively likes people and is eager to build friendships, sometimes with complete strangers. So the active will readily respond to any comments about similar backgrounds and the opportunity to share some information about himself.

The passive candidate is typically a little slower to respond. He is naturally inclined to express concern and interest in others but is slow to do so. If late for the appointment, he is the most likely to apologize sincerely for his tardiness. He most wants to be reassured about the process, and so he may interpret the initial rapport-building process as important and a genuine sense of interest in him. Thus, he may want to spend more time on establishing your mutual base of experiences to feel more comfortable with you during the actual interview process.

The sensitized candidate can be the easiest to categorize in the initial stages of the interview. He may appear shy and weakly extend a hand that is moist with perspiration. He is inclined to avoid eye contact with you and may have some difficulty if you stare intently at him. Your very first, most immediate impressions of him may be negative; however, it is wise to hold these in abeyance because if he is intelligent and if you can establish some rapport with him and lead him to a discussion of a topic that is both job-relevant and interesting to him, his job-related skills can become immediately apparent. So when a candidate shows limited eye contact, it is not necessarily a limiting factor on his candidacy. It does suggest that he may be sensitized and that you may need to be aware of that. He may have the social style of the sensitized person, but his technical skills may be so outstanding that he will be a real credit to any function.

The aggressive candidate can be somewhat domineering and potentially intimidating from the beginning of the interview. He prefers to be in charge and may look for ways to influence the interview. He likes to think in terms of control and predicting the outcome of any event, and so under the pressure of an interview he may be somewhat pushy and forceful. He will accept your attempts at rapport building and generally will respond positively to suggestions of similarity in your backgrounds.

If he sees you as being a kindred spirit, for example, a fellow college athlete or someone interested in sports, then he will see you as a potential ally and will be more inclined to relax and be himself with you. The active will look for, and respond to, genuine expressions of friendship, whereas the aggressive will see you as a potential comrade-in-arms. This distinction may be subtle, but it is telling about the two different behavior types.

The compulsive type is generally rare in the population and difficult to recognize easily in the initial stages of the interview. He may come with a prepared set of notes about himself or a list of questions he would like to ask during the interview. A sense of organization and methodical attention to detail typify this candidate, and he will appreciate the sense of organization and order you bring to the interview.

Introduction

After you establish some rapport with the candidate, you need to tell him that you would like to ask him some questions about his background to gain a better understanding of him as a candidate for the position.

The introduction is listed as a separate section because it represents an important line of demarcation between building rapport and beginning the actual interview. In essence, you are saying, "OK, now that we are friends, I want to begin to ask you some semipersonal questions." The understanding is that the questions are job-related and focused on obtaining a better understanding of the candidate as a person, but still you are communicating that this stage is the beginning of the interview process. Actually, of course, you have been evaluating the candidate since you first met him, but you are now simply saying that you want to build on the presumed friendship you have established in the past 5 to 10 minutes you have chatted.

The individual behavior traits do not typically respond to this statement in any specific fashion. Sometimes, however, a candidate will respond with a comment or mannerism that is reflective of this type. For example, the entrepreneur may say, "Great, that's what I'm here for" and glance up at you to gauge your reaction to his anticipation of the real beginning of the interview, perceived by him as a contest. The active may say, with an uplifting tone and sense of semiurgency, "OK, let's get started," reflecting his desire to expend some energy. The passive person may say simply, "Fine," while the sensitized, realizing the pressure may begin to mount now, may merely look aside for a second and not respond at all. Each of these behaviors is possible and merely indicative of behaviors that each of the traits may demonstrate at this junction in the interview.

PART 2: BACKGROUND

Many of the responses in this section have been covered in chapter 4; it is suggested that you review that chapter for additional insights into the responses to these questions.

Early Childhood

By definition, early childhood can be a sensitive area about which to be asking questions; however, asking about a candidate's early life history is not for the sake of prying into the historical or emotional past. Genuine, valid reasons exist to ask about this time in a person's life to obtain information that relates to his emotional development. Little information is gained here that can be used alone categorically to define the candidate's overall behavior style or interpersonal skill level, but information and insights are gained here that can lay the groundwork for understanding the candidate's later behavior.

For example, the person who says, "We were dirt-poor and lived a day-to-day existence—and so I was determined never to worry about money again" is telling you something about his most basic motives. Information that you gain later from him may suggest that this experience led him to become

- highly disciplined and controlled, to control and influence his own environment (suggesting an overachiever orientation)
- competitive, driven, and eager for success at almost any cost (possible entrepreneur)
- determined to have a steady, reliable, predictable job with regular salary increases and a 20-year retirement party with a gold watch (probably passive)

The point is that his early life experiences influenced him to do something and act in a certain manner. By exploring the person's life in this way, we can discover some basic whys and wherefores for his current behavior.

Some research has been completed on the importance of birth order in the family, for example, the oldest child versus the youngest child. This general research area needs to be refined further before definitive statements can be made about the importance of birth order as it relates to the development of behavior styles. Asking a candidate about his birth order and his relations with his siblings, however, can give you insights into how he sees this factor affecting his development. The person who says, "We were emotionally close and still are" may be hinting at a different kind of development from the person who says, "We all went different directions and I don't see them very often." By themselves these comments can seem nonproductive but they can lead to discussions about other areas like friendship and commitment that are meaningful in measuring a person's interpersonal skills.

Education

Educational experiences, especially high school and college, can be very revealing about the candidate's behavior style. Most entrepreneurs competed in some form of organized athletics in high school and/or college. They were not necessarily the star player, first string, or even lettered in the sport; however, they competed at some level and thoroughly enjoyed the experience. As adults they probably follow some favorite team and can discuss some aspect of their favorite sport or game at some length.

While more intelligent students generally received better grades in high school and college, achievement-oriented adults also like the idea of being graded in school. High overachiever, entrepreneur, and aggressive persons will take some pride in tangible achievements they attained in school. Grades (when controlling for natural intelligence) are one indication of this form of measured achievement. Participation in athletics is another.

The question sometimes arises whether, for example, C grades from an Ivy League university are better than B grades from a state university or whether C grades with an engineering major are better than B grades with a history major. In general, it is important to remember that many research studies show that almost no correlation exists between grades (from any institution or major) and success in a career. Grades, however, are one indication of how hard a student was willing to work to achieve some measure of competence.

Generally, the grades a student received should be compared with the immediate environment in which they were obtained; that is, student grade achievement behavior, like water, tends to seek its own level. The more the student wants and pressures himself to achieve higher grades, the more he will work for them. Grades should be compared as grades. A grade of B suggests a more disciplined interest in school than a grade of C, no matter what the candidate's college major or institution. Certainly areas of specialization can be indicative of relative intelligence.

There is some correlation between college major and behavior trait. The sensitized and compulsive traits, who are also highly intelligent, frequently major in engineering and physical science. Physical education attracts some individuals who are more inclined to be active and/or aggressive. These are gross categorizations and need to be cross-checked with why a candidate selected a specific college major. For example, the person whose college major is finance may have an entrepreneurial inclination, but the candidate who majored in finance and who says, "I majored in finance because I wanted to learn the technical terms of money making, get a job on Wall Street, and make my own fortune" is, in this one statement, indicating a strong entrepreneurial bent. Whether he possesses the self-discipline actually to accomplish this goal may require additional study, but this one statement suggests he leans in that direction.

Work Experience

The work experience section is probably the most critical part of the interview in terms of both gaining meaningful information from the candidate about his interpersonal skills and evaluating him technically for the position. Evaluating a candidate's interpersonal skills by reviewing his responses to this section also largely involves reviewing both the responses to the questions in chapter 3 and the section on temperament in this chapter.

It is almost impossible for the interviewer to be technically aware of the nuances of every position. A reasonable approach, however, is to ask the candidate to explain in rudimentary terms what he does and how he accomplished it. Generally, the more effectively the person can explain the functions of his current and past positions the more capably he satisfied their requirements.

To guard against a candidate's significant exaggeration of his past responsibilities, you can ask him to explain in detail exactly his responsibilities in the overall task that was accomplished. Sometimes such requests for increasingly specific accountability will cause a candidate to rephrase his answers from "I oversaw the total function of . . ." to something less inclusive like "I participated in [with a team of peers] the accomplishment of . . ."

The overachiever is inclined to state the facts of his employment fairly directly and in an uncomplicated manner. When asked for clarification on his duties, he will not reduce the originally stated scope of his responsibilities but will provide increasing amounts of detail of just how he accomplished a given task. He will not be insulted, annoyed, or frustrated at your asking. He will generally be pleased that you want to know more of his operations, and he will be pleased to share a review of his accomplishments with you. "After all," he would objectively think to himself, "I was asked to talk about myself, so I did."

The work history of the entrepreneur will likely revolve around individual accomplishments, or group accomplishments where he can claim a significant role. The reason is that the entrepreneurial trait is effective at completing tasks that require the skills of a unique person (like individual sales) or a small team of specialists. On the negative side, he is inclined to overstate the results, with a particular emphasis on his unique contribution to the overall success of the operation. The entrepreneur frequently associates himself with any organizational success but quickly denies any knowledge of a program that fails.

If success has a thousand fathers, then the entrepreneur will generally claim to be one of them, but he is just as quick to abandon the orphan task whose very conception was a mistake. When obviously caught in overstating his role in a particular project, the entrepreneur is inclined to assume that he misunderstood the original question and say, "Oh, I didn't mean that I was in charge of the whole project. It was a $10-million deal, and my role was more of a consultant and facilitator."

The active readily admits his preference for working in groups and has almost no difficulty sharing the responsibility and credit for task accomplishment. The higher the overachiever and active traits in the candidate, however, the more he is eager to state that he was responsible for some particular portion of the task, although the overall group completed the entire project. He may describe himself as a strong team player who played a significant role but was part of a larger organization. He may then emphasize that to accomplish anything of significant size requires a well-organized team effort and that he was an important contributor to the overall team accomplishment.

The high passive candidate may indicate his role on a team effort in a manner similar to that of the high active candidate, but he will be much slower to suggest his individual contribution or accomplishments. He is generally much happier projecting himself as a contributing team member, but not necessarily a critical contributor, especially if he is pushed or asked to clarify his exact role in a particular assignment.

The sensitized candidate will frequently understate his contribution. Remember, he is somewhat shy and self-effacing and tends to think of talking about his accomplishments as foolish boasting that, in general, makes him uncomfortable. So if you suspect that the candidate is technically quite capable, ask him to elaborate on his role. The more he feels comfortable talking about his accomplishments, the more he will discuss them.

In a fashion the sensitized is almost the exact opposite of the entrepreneur. The entrepreneur can claim more credit than he legitimately deserves and ultimately but frequently backs down from his original claims of broad success. The sensitized will fully acknowledge the scope of his contribution only after repeated requests for it. To the sensitized person's way of thinking, he knows that he accomplished the task and that this accomplishment is most important; the interviewer should be able to understand that point without prying too hard. If the interviewer asks, however, he will explain just how he completed each step of the process.

The compulsive candidate is very proud of his systematic manner and orderly, methodical, and precise habits in completing almost any job. The type of work is almost inconsequential to him. He simply brings a strong sense of order and precision to any task. The person who demonstrates this fairly rarely seen pure trait will generally be obvious to the interviewer.

Activities

The responses to this set of questions can be indicative of the behavior traits and generally supply additional evidence for a person's probable trait.

The overachiever will discuss some outside activities but will also stress the fact that he is so burdened with responsibilities to work, family, and community that he has little time to enjoy his personal and private pleasures. His orientation is toward the responsibility of commitment. So although many people will mention participation or membership in a given group, he will readily list the group's agendas, policies, and accomplishments. He does not join groups for the sake of socializing but to accomplish some specific purpose. In some ways, he feels obligated, by donating time to a specific cause, to repay someone for something he thinks he received, hence a membership or hobby that is outside his normal workday activity.

The entrepreneur can be a solid sports fan and hence may be a regular at professional sports events. For example, he may hold season tickets to the games of a professional sports team, or he may be a regular golfer and country club member. He enjoys being with, around, and part of some group of people whom he may describe as in some way elite. Not everyone who regularly attends a given sports event or belongs to a country club is automatically an entrepreneur; however, these types of activities—with the possibility for an emphasis on competitive winning, with success dependent on personal skill, with the opportunity for an occasional friendly wager on the outcome of either a golf game or sports event, and with the implied status of playing at the country club—are typical of the entrepreneurial person.

The active candidate will also show a number of outside activities, and during a discussion of them he will emphasize the importance of his friendships at these associations. He may admit that he is overcommitted and finds it difficult to attend all the meetings and that he intends to reduce the number of his obligations. He will be slow, however, to admit significant responsibility for specific accomplishments within any of the groups. He participates with such groups primarily because of the chance to be with old buddies and the opportunity to make new friends.

The passive candidate is somewhat similar to the active person in that he too can belong to some groups. He tends to join work-related groups with the stated purpose of learning more about his profession. These memberships reflect his willingness to join popular, well-meaning, socially approved activities, but his number of association memberships will be smaller than that of the active person. Another difference is that he will emphasize that he has little time for any of the meetings. He may hold an office in one such group but will complain about the amount of time required to maintain the functions. His position in such groups is seldom a leadership role but may emphasize activities like record keeping or maintenance of some accounts.

The sensitized seldom joins social organizations. He may, however, belong to a chess club, science fiction club, or reading club. His stated purpose in joining any of these clubs will be more for intellectual development than for companionship or interpersonal needs.

The aggressive candidate may list a wide range of clubs or associations. Typically, however, he will be active in a few and will readily explain his plan to become an officer and eventually president of one. The aggressive person is motivated by the notion of social power and is eager to hold a position of leadership in many of the social groups to which he belongs. He wants to be in charge and sees himself as being well suited for a position of overall leadership. Hence, he frequently either currently occupies or plans to hold a position of leadership in his social group.

The activities section provides little insight into the compulsive candidate, although the order, sequence, and generally systematic approach in answering the questions will provide some clues.

Self-Description

The response to this question can provide you significant additional information to understand and define the candidate. By this time in the interview you should have some general impressions of the candidate, and his answer to this question can enable you to confirm or double-check some of those impressions.

The overachiever will discuss himself in a straightforward manner and be fairly objective in describing both his accomplishments and his failures, although he may describe them more easily if they are referred to as setbacks rather than failures. The consistent theme in his responses to this set of questions frequently is overcoming obstacles, achieving rewards, and learning about himself from many of the situations he faced. For example, he may indicate that a particular employment position was a mistake, but he will also frequently mention that he learned what not to do next time and that he has avoided that kind of situation since then. The overachiever person includes a feedback mechanism that enables him to self-correct for having made what he considers mistakes in judgment.

The entrepreneur may take either of two tracks in response to this question. He may start to reply in a humble manner, with words to the effect that he has not really accomplished much but that he has done a few things of which he is proud. At this point he will go on to extol the virtues of his accomplishments. Or he will directly, possibly in a conceited manner, list his accomplishments, which may in fact be quite impressive. His manner of listing his record of successes can be off-putting to others.

He may have some trouble admitting mistakes or be inclined to blame others for his misfortune. A frequent comment about failures starts with "If I only hadn't trusted X to hold up his end of the bargain," or he may say that at one point he either was wealthy or was on the verge of being really wealthy, but some last-minute detail went wrong, and so now he is interviewing for this job. That is, the entrepreneur tends to paint himself in a light more glorious than the facts suggest is realistic.

The active candidate is happy to discuss himself and is pleased to summarize his accomplishments, and he will do so in an upbeat and positive manner, but also with surprising candor and honesty. In relaying his accomplishments, he may tend to err on the side of positive exaggeration, but this is more from enthusiasm than from a desire to deceive anyone. He will probably emphasize his sense of energy and history of long hours on a given job. "I am not afraid to work" is a typical comment from the active.

He will comment that others describe him as enthusiastic and even driven to meet his goals, and he will use these same words to describe himself. He will admit to a desire for additional training, but he may also add that he does not seem to have time to do it. For example, he may currently be halfway through a series of courses for some professional designation. This state of affairs reminds one of the well-intentioned but sometimes overburdened schedule he keeps; he means quite well but can promise too many people too much of his time.

The passive candidate will describe his successes and failures in much more muted terms than does the active. He tends not to reach as high as other people but also takes care to cover his risks when he does venture out beyond his structured life. He will see significant risks and major accomplishments in terms of group activities in which he participated. At the same time, he may see a failure in terms of some personal frustration that was due to bad luck or some factor beyond his control. In general, however, his notion of success and failure is much more restricted than the notion of others.

He is inherently cautious and much prefers structure and definition to the inherently unstructured activities that generally lead to significant accomplishment or ready failure. For example, he may cite his finishing of some structured program like an M.B.A. (completed four years ago, over a three-year period at night) or some other formal training program as a significant success. Admittedly, completing such programs is a success, but typically successful people will have something more recent to mention.

The sensitized candidate may have some difficulty talking comfortably about himself. His natural hesitancy to describe himself may be another indication of his behavior trait. When prodded, however, he will describe accomplishments in a general and factual manner but with an honestly self-effacing tone. For example, he is inclined to describe a college-level organic chemistry course as "mostly memorization." Gaining an accurate understanding of him may require the significant use of your social skills.

This question can provide the aggressive candidate the opportunity he has been seeking to list his accomplishments. Remember, this person is proud of his record on most subjects and is eager to share positive information about himself. He is typically somewhat emotionally insecure and afraid; however, by comparing himself to others and by generally defining himself as better in such comparisons, he feels more secure and pleased with himself. So he can welcome this set of questions as an opportunity to list the many functions he has headed and the groups he has led to success. Just as the entrepreneur will tend to focus on feats of individual accomplishment, the aggressive candidate will favor activities that require group leadership. Hence, his greatest accomplishments will include self-described dynamic leadership and reflect a socially aggressive, take-charge attitude.

The highly compulsive candidate may show this tendency in terms of his orderly presentation and possibly matter-of-fact listing of the facts about his life. He tends not to be emotional, and although fully cooperative in the sense of supplying information to your questions, he is not necessarily highly responsive to attempts at engaging him in more general conversational topics.

PART 3: TEMPERAMENT

The trait topics described in this section are intended to refine further the evaluation of a given candidate when compared with the requirements of a specific position. These questions are designed to be asked either as an integral portion (follow-up questions) of background questions or as a separate set of questions.

The traits discussed in the chapter are defined as follows:

Planning and organizing. Is systematic, methodical, and well prepared for his activities. He first plans his activities and then generally follows the plan to accomplish the ends he has in mind. Creating the plan is perceived to be an important part of the achievement process.

Problem analysis. Intelligent. Lays out a comprehensive strategy and then can identify and discuss specific tactics to achieve his goals.

Judgment and decisiveness. Acts and reacts quickly to situations but, when pressed, can state the facts of the situation and describe his thinking process (how he evaluated the situation) in making a decision. So he is quick to decide but thorough in his analysis.

Risk taking. Strong evidence that the candidate believes in betting (e.g. the lottery or on games of complete chance) and expects to win. The person, however, may bet on himself in terms of beating another person in a sporting event (e.g. golf or bowling) or in terms of his ability to predict the outcome of some sporting event in which he does not participate, such as professional athletics.

Delegation. Allows, encourages, and believes in pushing down work to the furthest possible level so that the lower-level personnel are forced to learn and the higher-level personnel can/must do more creative work and in turn continually push it down to others.

Follow-up and control. Checks to make sure that each *i* is dotted and *t* crossed to ensure the proper functioning of a given project. Exercises appropriate level of supervision of staff to facilitate work flow.

Drive. Pushes self to achieve whatever goals he or his boss sets or implies that he should reach.

Self-esteem. Likes himself and believes in his contribution to the overall effort. Yet not obviously conceited or narcissistic about his past accomplishments.

Self-development. Interested in further developing his professional, personal, and other abilities as they relate to the job. Sees self-development as an important part of maintaining his level of expertise.

Stress tolerance. Capable of handling ambiguous situations that are not complete. Able to deal with a lack of structure and informal rules rather than a clearly defined hierarchy. Accustomed to making decisions with incomplete information and operates well in a changing environment.

Adaptability. Flexible and accepts change readily. Understands that sometimes "things happen" and that he must adapt to the situation.

Persuasiveness. Able to convince others that he has the optimal, best, or right point of view. Brings others around to his manner of thinking about a given topic.

Communication. Speaks clearly and completely about any topic under discussion. Expresses his thoughts in a complete (written) format and uses reasonable (introductory comment, descriptive comments, summary comment) structure in response to questions about given situations.

These topics are generic subjects that candidates for a variety of positions requiring a certain amount of interpersonal skill are frequently rated on during an interview. Presenting them here, however, in the context of analyzing them with references to the seven behavior traits enables us to understand better each candidate's interpersonal strengths and weaknesses.

The importance of using the traits presented in this section along with the seven traits defined in chapter 1 can be illustrated with reference to some of the traits. Let's start with drive. This trait can be defined in a number of ways that are valid; however, it may be best defined when used in conjunction with some of the seven behavior traits.

Some of the ways that drive can be defined in conjunction with the seven traits are:

Overachiever

Self-discipline to attain a self-defined goal of accomplishing a task or reaching a single achievement.

Entrepreneur

Competitive to win a sales contest, make more money, or gain a perk that defines some higher form of executive status.

Active

Emotional enthusiasm to win friends and build a team effort around a given project.

Passive

A stated desire for structure, definition, and rules to work by (low drive), indicating a more submissive and cautious approach.

Aggressive

Domineering, authoritative, and determined to convince others on the shop floor, in the factory, or in the corporate boardroom.

Sensitized

A history of working alone but achieving significant goals without support from, or participation in, group activities. Sets and reaches goals that are important to him, despite an apparent lack of reinforcement from any tangible source. Internally driven to achieve because the goal has personal meaning for him.

Compulsive

The stated desire and demonstrated habit of finishing a number of activities simply because "a person should finish whatever he begins." No special pleasure in finishing for some form of reward, but just for the sake of finishing.

So, in rating a candidate's level of drive, we should both note the level of the drive and further explain it in terms of one or more of the seven traits. Let's assume that we rate a given individual high on the trait drive. Now we need to note the sort of drive and how it is reflected in terms of the seven traits.

Another example of how the seven traits listed in chapter 1 and the traits listed in this chapter complement each other can be seen in reviewing the trait persuasiveness.

Overachiever

Oftentimes is considered persuasive primarily because he is logical, rational, orderly, and systematic. The statement "The logic of his argument was overwhelming" reflects this kind of overachiever persuasiveness.

Entrepreneur

Frequently is considered persuasive because he is very clever at reading his audience and can quickly tailor his presentation to fit the perceived and immediate needs of the audience.

Active

Sometimes is considered persuasive because he is so emotional, pleasant, genuinely well meaning, and obviously sincere that he is difficult to refuse.

Passive

Typically easily led and influenced by others (low persuasiveness). He will be sympathetic and possibly influenced by whoever speaks to him last.

Aggressive

Frequently is perceived to be persuasive because he is socially relentless, individually domineering, and almost insists on presenting his material.

Sensitized

Generally viewed as being nonpersuasive in the social sense of the word but is highly ethical and moved to act on principle. If, for example, during a public debate he decides that X is the proper course of action, then others might be swayed to follow him.

Compulsive

Sometimes is perceived to be persuasive because he is so logical, factual, and almost devoid in emotionality in presenting his ideas. That is, the compulsive by definition is not emotional, and so his ideas can be perceived as especially straightforward and "no-nonsense."

To facilitate the process of thinking of these dimensions and the seven behavior traits when interviewing/evaluating someone for a position, consider using Chart 6.1. The dimensions are listed on the left, a rating scheme is listed across the top of the graph, and a space is left for you to fill in with comments concerning your impressions of the candidate's level of a particular dimension. At this time, you can also make some notes about how the candidate's score on this dimension is related to one of the seven behavior traits.

Planning and Organizing

Look over the 120 Questionnaire and get a feeling for the individual. In the margins, make observations about how the person addressed himself to the task of completing the form.

A high degree of planning and organizing (P & O) is naturally associated with a high measure of the overachiever. By definition this person is plan-oriented, disciplined, organized, and concerned with achieving his goals—regardless of reward—in an organized and controlled fashion. The emphasis here is on achieving goals. The overachiever sees accomplishment of any task assigned him as being highly important, and he is concerned to complete it in a precise and professional manner. His 120 Questionnaire responses will reflect this concern for efficiency and neatness.

The entrepreneur, on the other hand, is more concerned with completing a task for a specific financial reward. Time is money to this person, and he may indicate during the interview that he did not have sufficient time to complete the 120 Questionnaire completely or as thoroughly as he would have liked. He is likely to leave some portion (e.g., the work history section, which asks specifically about salary history) incomplete with the words "see resume" written across it.

The active person is the most likely to provide the most information about himself. He likes to communicate and, if he has reasonable intelligence and writing skills, he will typically provide the most written volume. He may also provide answers that you might interpret as very personal and candid. He is inclined to include names of people, although names are not specifically requested. This behavior is simply expressive of his sense of social sharing.

The passive person's written responses will be neat, orderly, and clearly defined. In this regard, the responses can appear similar to the responses of the overachiever and the compulsive. At the same time, the responses of the passive can be somewhat mixed and even cluttered; that is, the questionnaire may be completed in differently colored inks or be completed partially in ink and partially in pencil. This style will probably reflect that the person started and stopped doing the questionnaire and used whatever pen or pencil was readily available at the time that he started working on it. To some degree,

Chart 6.1
Candidate Trait Chart

Candidate Name _____

Trait Name		Comments
10-20	Rapport/Intro	
30	Early Childhood	
40	Education	
50	Work Experiences	
60	Activities	
70	Self-Description	
80	Planning and Organizing	
90	Problem Analysis	
100	Judgment and Decisiveness	
110	Risk Taking	
120	Delegation	
130	Follow-Up and Control	
140	Drive	
150	Self-Esteem	
160	Self-Development	
170	Stress Tolerance	
180	Adaptability	
190	Persuasiveness	
200	Communication	
210-220	Info/Conclusion	
Summary Comments		

this lack of consistency (switching between pen and pencil) reflects a low overachiever and compulsive.

The aggressive tends to see glory and possibly increased status and social recognition for achieving his tasks, including completing the 120 Questionnaire. The form and style he uses to complete the questionnaire provide few cues as to his identity.

The sensitized person can be intimidated and even annoyed at the prospect of completing the questionnaire. He may remark that some parts of it are too personal or that he does not see where the questions are necessarily job-related. He is especially likely to leave some of the sentence completion items blank, but he will not necessarily state in writing why he is doing so. As indicated above, the entrepreneur will leave the questions regarding his salary history blank because this is personal information to him. The sensitized person, however, will provide answers to these factual questions but fail to respond to ones that he sees as prying into his mental/emotional attitudes.

Compulsive responses will typically be neat, orderly, and, in some cases, incredibly detailed.

The following list provides some indicators for the dimension of planning and organizing.

120 Questionnaire. Neat and orderly presentation of facts and ideas. Organization and presentation of data are clear.

Past employment. Look for evidence of P & O on the job. Determine how much of his effort was dictated or planned and organized by him. Some jobs require more P & O than others, for example, outside sales versus computer operator. Look for evidence of planning in his reasons for changing jobs.

Education. Early identification of a major area of study versus several changes. Taking elective courses to prepare for work. Supporting himself while getting his education. Involvement in multiple activities. Delaying family until education is completed. Saving money, buying life insurance. Work history is consistent with education preparation.

Military. Note activities and what he liked most and least about his military experience.

Extracurricular activities. Look for evidence of P & O in the kind of activities he was interested in or in the positions he held. For example, debating requires more P & O than social club, but social chairman probably requires more P & O than just being a member.

Plans for the future. Most people do not have specific, step-by-step plans, but some have determined a direction and have reasons for it. "Get sales experience" is better than "Get a job."

Interview. Is on time, is prepared for interview, knows about the company. Responses are clear and show evidence of organization; for example, the response to "What is success to you?" may be "Three things are important: one, achievement at work; two, family; three, money."

Problem Analysis

To evaluate problem analysis (PA) skills, as in the other areas, we concern ourselves with what can be observed. We cannot measure the ability but, rather, the use of that ability.

The process of determining an individual's problem analysis skills presents a challenge to the interviewer, primarily because the observations are not as direct and one must learn to interpret what he hears. Assessing PA skills, as well as judgment and decisiveness, is dependent upon determining the whys and wherefores of a person's behavior, rather than simply observing or noting an action.

No doubt there is some relationship between intelligence and problem analysis skills, but we are not going to measure intelligence. We are going to make the assumption, however, that people who conduct themselves in more intelligent ways generally display better problem analysis skills.

To determine PA skills, we are going to look at some ways in which the individual expresses himself intelligently, as well as some ways in which the individual seeks out pertinent data and determines the source and key dimensions of a problem.

Intelligence can be defined as the ability to learn, to understand new concepts, to perceive relationships, and to solve problems. Intelligent people tend to understand instructions more readily, and they are usually able to communicate ideas more clearly and more simply. They tend to think more logically and often have more reasons for doing the things they do. Many highly intelligent people, however, make stupid business decisions. By the same token, many people who turn in a stellar performance academically behave poorly in business. So we are not necessarily looking for highly intelligent people but rather for those who can use their ability to make sensible judgments and discriminations on practical work problems.

Lack of intelligence is revealed by interview responses that are dull, incomplete, or too literal; that indicate faulty perception or lack of reasoning power; or that suggest a very restricted horizon, with little understanding of self, other people, or the world in general.

The ways in which people express themselves are an indication of their intelligence. From the 120 Questionnaire and interview, we can look for clues in the individual's presentation of facts, the form in which they are presented, and the content of what is said.

Age at high school graduation is a fact. In general but not always, those who graduated at age 16 or 17 are likely to be brighter than those who graduated at 19 or 20.

Form is the way in which facts are presented. An example is the way a candidate writes dates, places, and names. One may consistently abbreviate (Grover Mfg. Co., Phil., PA) while another consistently spells out words in full; the latter is probably more detail-oriented, but, of course, he may be overly concerned with details, a trait that may be good or bad, depending on the job. Attention to detail per se is typically a function of the overachiever, passive, and/or compulsive behavior style. The problem analysis dimension, however, is to assist you in determining intelligence, rather than personality traits.

Content refers to the idea or meaning contained in the response and in the way it is expressed. For example, a person who indicates that his former employer was a manufacturer is not as good a communicator as one who says, "Manufacturer of custom kitchen and storage cabinets." Consider a response to the question "What are your plans for the future?" In terms of perspective on life, "Get a job and get married" is not as good a response as "Get a job as a machinist apprentice, study, and learn with the hope of advancement."

It is exceedingly important to be careful about making such generalizations. They can be meaningful, but they are only clues and must be evaluated in light of other facts and the total picture of the applicant.

The following list summarizes some indicators of superior versus average intelligence in a candidate.

General

Superior: Complete responses. Clear and precise communication. Adding more data than space allows.

Average: Misinterpretation of instructions. Minimal or unclear communication. Grammar and spelling errors.

Liked Most About Former Jobs

Superior: Responses that show grasp of work and how his work was important to company and/or indicate pleasure in learning, solving problems, and achieving.

Average: General responses like "meeting people," "liked all of it," "pleasant surroundings."

Job Description

Superior: Well organized and communicates function and responsibilities.

Average: General; poor communication; simple list of duties.

Subjects in School

Superior: As a rule, English, math, physical sciences, and languages are the more difficult and analytical subjects.

Average: Hygiene and civics are easier subjects. Bookkeeping, typing, shop, and drafting are very literal subjects.

Extracurricular Activities

Superior: Variety of activities, especially debating, science club, honor society, student council.

Average: No extracurricular activities or all in one area, for example, only sports.

Hobbies or Interests

Superior: Intellectual (reading, TV documentaries, numismatic or philatelist clubs); sports participant; competes with standards (golf, bowling) or with others individually (tennis, racquetball); variety of interests; unusual interests considering background.

Average: Recreational; sports spectator; primarily group activities (square dancing, choral singing); limited or no nonwork interests.

Part-Time Jobs When Younger

Superior: Jobs that require some initiative like selling or starting a small business (lawn work or food concession).

Average: Stockboy, clerk, or no jobs.

Kind of Vacation Preferred

Superior: "Travel and see new places," family camping.

Average: More literal: "summer" or "two weeks."

Qualifications for a More Responsible Position

Superior: However it is phrased, some mention of ability and desire to learn or willingness to undertake new responsibility suggests an open and receptive mind.

Average: "Past experience" or "Have always done well on any task assigned" suggests a more literal and less responsive mind.

Selection of College and Course of Study

Superior: Evidence of analysis, judgment, logic, and reasoning behind selection; made selections himself; determined course of study.

Average: Attended close to home or where family went; took others' suggestions; took courses until found interest.

Judgment and Decisiveness

No new questions need to be added to determine decisiveness and judgment. Judgment is the ability to draw logical conclusions based upon established evidence.

Some people display poor judgment. Some people, in an effort to meet their needs or to accomplish their purposes, ignore the evidence available or fail to establish evidence. More often, however, poor problem analysis is the culprit, rather than an inability to draw logical conclusions based on established evidence. To determine judgment, simply look for the logic behind the person's decisions.

Evaluate the decisions the person has made in the areas you have already discussed. How did he go about making them? Did he decide for himself, or did someone decide for him? On this dimension we are more concerned with his willingness to choose from among alternatives than with the quality of the decision. In other words, it is possible that a person can be very decisive but will make poor decisions as a result of poor problem analysis.

In addition to a willingness to select from among alternatives and a readiness to render judgment, there are some other characteristics that tend to denote decisiveness. More decisive people, as well as more intelligent people, tend to respond to questions more quickly. When open-ended questions are posed, these people will decide how they are going to respond rather than constantly ask for clarification. They tend to be able to shift subjects more quickly in response to questions. They are as definite in their responses to opinion questions as they are to factual questions.

The overachiever, as a general rule, exercises both good judgment and reasonable decisiveness. He will carefully measure the facts of a situation and, depending on other factors in his personality, generally decide to proceed with some rational plan of advancement. Most of all, he has rationally planned his arguments and will follow a decided path to achieve his goals.

The entrepreneur typically will act with reasonable judgment and decisiveness but is also inclined to look out for himself along the way, so he will emphasize results that will favor his position or individual advancement. He is not afraid to endorse a given plan of action, and if the idea is successful, he may look to grab a large share of the credit. If it fails, however, he may be quickest to abandon any association with it.

The active is quick to be excited about an idea, and this sense of enthusiasm may cloud his judgment. Moreover, he may waffle about actually making a final decision. Frequently the active is better at coming up with a number of exciting possibilities but then has some difficulty choosing the proper alternative.

The passive person, on the other hand, will take a very conservative viewpoint and may balk at making any decision. His judgment will be solid but frequently is highly conservative—again, he is afraid of making mistakes.

The sensitized person can be quite decisive and difficult to change once he has made up his mind. He may pay some form of lip service to other ideas but will subtly and persistently hold onto his own. His judgment is typically quite good, but he will not act in an outwardly decisive manner.

The aggressive person will be so decisive that he will implement whatever decision he judges to be correct. Like a train crossing the prairie, the aggressive person travels straight ahead. He will flatly, openly, and steadfastly defend his decisions. Sometimes this behavior can be categorized as "holding the course"; at other times, it may appear as simple stubbornness and inflexibility. Oftentimes the final evaluation will depend on whether the decision resulted in success or failure.

Risk Taking

The problem with risk taking is that it is difficult to determine on a consistent basis whether taking a risk is good or bad. The judgment is usually external and relative. In other words, if a risk is taken, and it works out well, people consider it good; if not, it is bad. Similar observations can be made about not taking a risk. It is generally true, however, that the higher you go in management, the greater the risks; hence, a manager has to be willing to accept risk. There are several kinds of risk takers.

In an ideal setting the overachiever realizes the need to take risks and is willing to take them. He has learned to have confidence in his analysis skills and can move ahead even when all the facts are not known. He knows he is placing himself in a vulnerable position and is willing to do so because the potential gain outweighs the consequences. He weighs alternatives, and his decisions are timely. The overachiever collects data, analyzes well, is willing to ask others for their opinions, makes decisions as rapidly as necessary, and is adaptable and learns from his mistakes.

The entrepreneur displays a high level of independence and autonomy. He is intent on doing things the way that will pay off most quickly. He may show a low regard for rules, policy, and procedures. He may or may not be aware of risk. It does not matter to him because he is going to do what he wants to do when he wants to do it. He strives to be unique and different. He is trying to make a personal statement to those around him, a statement that says that he is betting on himself. His actions can be the ultimate act of foolish bravado. His thinking can follow the lines that if he is involved in a project, it will surely work and that he believes in himself and his ability to take a calculated risk.

At the same time, the entrepreneur is the most likely person to have an emergency trapdoor established for him to escape blame for the project if it fails. He is not so much concerned with a contingency plan to save the operation or anyone else associated with it, but he will have prepared an alternative explanation or excuse for his involvement in the project. He will sit on the fence the longest and wait until clear indication exists about who or what will win the battle before he commits to a solid recommendation, and even then he will be prepared to dissociate himself from a negative result.

The active person is likely to see the situation as containing some risk, but he will think to himself, "Let's go for it." He may not consider all the ramifications of his actions, and he would be the first to admit that if he did think of everything that could go wrong, then he would never even attempt to act. In essence, he will ignore the possible negative consequences of his actions, not because he is malicious or conniving but because he refuses to allow negative thoughts to deter him from acting.

The passive person is exceedingly cautious and careful to the point that action is stymied. He places himself in a vulnerable position by virtue of taking no action. He fails to make a decision, even though the deadline is upon him. He is a fearful person, afraid to take action. His objective is to avoid mistakes at all costs. He is happier being told what to do than deciding what to do. He tries very hard to conjecture, anticipate, and predict but can never do so well enough to feel comfortable committing himself. His sins are ones of omission, not commission.

The sensitized is not aware that he is placing himself in a vulnerable position. He is somewhat rule-bound or experience-bound and may make decisions or take action without considering the pertinent data or source and key dimensions of the problem.

The aggressive person will frequently go to great lengths to provide social evidence that he is sure of himself, that is, he will work at selling his decision. Like an umpire who emphatically calls balls and strikes at a baseball game, the aggressive will leave no doubt about his convictions or beliefs. His judgment may not always be right, but he will emphatically deny the possibility that he is wrong, and he will believe that he is right.

Following is a list of indicators that distinguish high-risk from low-risk individuals. Remember, look for the individual who is able and willing to take a calculated risk. Some of the indicators may denote wild risk takers; use the description to distinguish them.

High risk. More willing to change jobs. Worked way through college. Left home early (by age 18). Married early (by age 20). Involved in a variety of extracurricular activities or has multiple interests. Makes own decisions. Venturesome. Independent. Confident. Extrovert. Competitive. Meets new people easily. Comfortable in unstructured environments. Seeks responsibility. Seeks challenge, achievement variety, opportunity to learn. Easily adjusts to change. Respects policy, rules, and values. Initiates activity.

Low risk. Few changes, may be security need. Supported by parents. Lived at home past age 23. Married later (after age 30). Fewer activities; intramural sports suggest more dependency. Follows instruction or suggestion. Cautious, careful. Dependent. Low self-esteem. Introvert. Less willing to be measured. Reserved with new people. Most comfortable in structured environments. Waits to be given responsibility. Seeks understanding, helpful superiors, supportive climate. Resists change. Rule-bound. Reacts to what happens.

Delegation

In general, a person who displays some planning and organization skills will have a leg up on others in learning to order and direct his own activities as well as the activities of others. Effective delegation, however, requires more. One must be able to delegate appropriately and therefore must be able to assess the skills of the individual to whom he is delegating. Once this individual is selected, the delegator must then be enough of a leader to motivate him to do the job and to do it well. Hence, there are many skills involved in effective delegation. Delegation has two main functions: to get the job done and to prepare individuals to take on broader responsibilities.

The ideal delegator is easy to identify. He is the person who understands the dual purpose of delegation. He delegates responsibilities, but, more importantly, he delegates authority. He understands the strengths and shortcomings of the individual to whom he delegates. He delegates not only to get the job done but also to develop his subordinates. He sees the necessity to prepare others to take on broader responsibilities. He has a longer range and broader view of his role as manager. He maintains control by following up on his subordinates. They report to him verbally and in writing. He evaluates their progress. He teaches them as well as criticizes them. He typically has confidence in others and feels that with the proper guidance they will raise their standards to meet his expectations.

Many of the behavior traits we are discussing have some of the characteristics of the ideal delegator described above; however, a quick review of some highlights of how each trait may delegate can be helpful in better understanding the traits.

The overachiever can be an effective delegator. As a rule he works hard, sets a good example, and unceremoniously leads others to achieve meaningful goals. He too, however, can have some problems in this area. He can set goals that seem reasonable to him but that may be too high for his subordinates to reach. He may assume that everyone is as task-oriented and self-disciplined as he and fail to monitor their activities. The overachiever will generally describe himself as a reasonable delegator of tasks, but he will also indicate that it is oftentimes necessary to double-check the work of others or even complete the work himself.

The entrepreneur is often pleased to delegate many task responsibilities, except the credit for their successful completion. He is frequently very able to size up others in terms of skills and abilities needed to complete a given assignment and to enlist their help in completing the job. He is an effective delegator and is proud of this ability. If asked about a project where he delegated some portion of the work and the task turned out badly, he may respond, "The only mistake I made was to trust those people to complete a simple assignment" and thereby imply that everything was set for a significant accomplishment but that some underling made a stupid mistake, which someone at his exalted level should not have to check.

The active will readily admit that he is capable of delegating a given task to trusted subordinates, but he will add that he is inclined to jump in and help them because he likes to be part of the action. The active has some difficulty removing himself from the activity that he is supposed to supervise. He does not necessarily interfere with the project or insist on being referred to as a working boss; he merely wants to be part of the team.

Individuals represented by the sensitized and compulsive behavior styles frequently are not effective delegators. Some of these people are not suited to supervise others because, among other things, they cannot or will not delegate. Some are reluctant to ask others to do things and if they did, would be poor at giving instructions. They certainly would not be able to deal effectively with a person who failed to complete the delegated assignment.

A passive can be an effective delegator. He will typically want to share the responsibility for a given decision and so is eager to share his work load. He will be compassionate, easygoing, and not demanding for analysis, until he begins to feel pressure from his boss for some results. Under that condition he can become harping, demanding, and critical of others; that is, he can be quick to criticize others and thereby compile evidence that their point of view is not justified. He is not so quick, however, to take the time to teach others to meet his expectations.

Conversely, some passives are poor delegators; these individuals want to do things themselves. From a positive point of view, they know what is going on. They are usually precise and give little leeway to subordinates. They are not good developers of people. They are cautious decision makers and have a low tolerance for risk. They usually plan and organize well and are thorough in their follow-through.

On the other hand, the sensitized may have little confidence in others and is therefore reluctant to delegate to them. His lack of confidence may or may not be related to the potential delegatee's competence. Some sensitized individuals also feel that no one can complete an assignment as well as they can, and so they do it themselves. They may do absolutely brilliant work, but there are limits to how much one person can complete on his own.

The highly aggressive person may wish to maintain all the control for himself and so becomes a task delegator; he assigns tasks rather than responsibility. This person realizes he has to have help to get the job done but has not yet learned to utilize people most effectively as resources. He usually assigns tasks according to the role the person plays or the position he holds rather than according to the individual's capabilities. The tasks are generally short-range or assigned one at a time and strictly for the purpose of getting the job done. This kind of delegator may not see or take responsibility for developing those under him.

Another aggressive kind of nondelegator is the person who has an exaggerated need for control and fears he will not be able to maintain control if he delegates to others. He is more comfortable working long hours to complete the work than he is supervising and teaching others. Capable, assertive people will not work long for this sort of manager because they derive very little job satisfaction. The people who will work for him are of the sort that will justify his belief that he is well advised to do the work himself. Other things being equal, this behavior alone will limit his span of control.

Now we will simply look at the existence or nonexistence of this skill. For present purposes, if an individual has had no experience delegating, we will assume he has no skill (this assumption may not be true, as delegation can be learned).

If the interviewee has had any experience where he could delegate (see list below), then his experience can be explored with him. Look at the following areas for possible delegation experiences:

- football quarterback
- team captain in any sport or activity
- coach of adolescent teams
- scout leader
- JCs' project leader
- coordinator of any volunteer activity
- play or drama director
- summer camp or park director

Follow-up and Control

Follow-up and control are the process of ensuring that directives have been understood and carried out. The process is not simple but is of paramount importance. As a manager increases his span of control, it is critical that he learn to exercise control without becoming bogged down with detail. Effective control requires the following:

- objective: describes what is to be accomplished
- procedure: specifies how, when, and by whom the plan is to be executed
- criterion: denotes what constitutes good performance
- appraisal: determines who well the job was done

Establishing objectives, policies, and procedures that are commonly understood will go a long way in establishing control. In addition, it is critical to establish standards of performance that indicate for each aspect of the procedure what constitutes good performance and how it is to be measured.

The above is the mechanism of exercising control. In addition, to appraise performance, the manager must establish evidence; in other words, he has to know what is going on. Follow-up or inspection provides the evidence needed. Some typical methods of follow-up are:

- on-site inspection
- verbal report in one-on-one meetings
- group reporting meetings for coordination
- written reports
- sign-off forms

Once again, if one has not been in a management or leadership position, he will have had no opportunity to develop this skill, and presumably the skill does not exist. This point is of little consequence, however, in assessing potential because techniques of follow-up and control can easily be learned.

For those who have been in a management or leadership position, we can explore their experience with them and evaluate the development of their skills in follow-up and control.

Obviously, those who possess basic planning and organization skills are more likely to appreciate the need for follow-up and control. This skill is closely tied to delegation; the manager who delegates effectively will quickly see the need to follow up.

The general behavior patterns of the seven behavior traits described in the section on delegation also apply to the behavior patterns associated with follow-up and control.

Drive

All people are motivated to accomplish something. They distinguish themselves by what they are after (direction of the drive) and how important it is to them (strength of the drive). To understand the strength of the drive, we need to determine how critical these decisions are, how long they have been acted upon, and how the individual hopes to act upon them in the future.

Following are a few of the common styles of motivations people display. They are included here simply for the reader's understanding of a few ways in which individuals categorized as variations of the seven traits can be distinguished. Think about each of these descriptions in terms of the implications for achievement and management.

Overachievers are rather independent and take pride in drawing on their own resources of intelligence, information, and experience. They may be difficult to influence or to lead. They enjoy having latitude within which to do things their own way. They rarely ask for assistance. Some find it difficult to accept criticism. They are typically highly ambitious. They want to achieve because achievement permits them independence. In addition, they often can achieve because they have developed confidence in themselves by relying on themselves. These people are often highly motivated in terms of both direction and strength of drive. Obviously, these people, through preference, practice, and experience, have learned to rely on themselves and not on others. They are usually decisive and risk-oriented. They are usually anxious to acquire skills (work or management) that will make them more self-reliant. They can become good managers.

Entrepreneurs are inclined to devote inordinate amounts of time to getting ahead. This interest may take the form of working long hours to gain a specific goal (bonus, commission, awards and so on). They tend to underestimate the significance of their present positions and believe that higher positions must of necessity be better. They are impressed by the trappings of office. They obviously have a strong drive to achieve, the direction of their motivation is to get ahead, and they are typically willing to learn or to do whatever is necessary to get ahead. They are knowledgeable of the rules of the game so as to be able to shortcut them if they can.

Typically, the entrepreneur learns to manage well but tends to look ahead at the expense of carefully attending to the tasks at hand. They often overemphasize the importance of looking good at the expense of being good. They learn to do many things well, including management, but will display impatience with activities that do not appear to advance their position. They are movers, initiators, and decision makers. They are, above all, results-oriented.

The active can appear to be either primarily strongly driven or merely interested in spending his energies. The actual behavior exhibited will typically depend upon the amount of the overachiever present along with the active. The higher the overachiever, the more purposeful the behavior of the active person. He will be friendly, sociable, well meaning, and concerned for the team welfare but also highly focused and concerned for the team to achieve a meaningful goal. He will work with the individual team members but will generally be regarded as the leader, not because he demands the position but because he is the logical choice.

The less the overachiever component in the highly active person, the more random (although equally highly energized) the person will appear. This person is ready, willing, and eager to help others but can be distracted from one activity and move to another quickly and may lose effectiveness because he honestly takes on more than he can meaningfully hope to finish.

Passive people attach a high importance to making sure that nothing goes awry. They are often good with detail and can anticipate difficulty long before it materializes. They leave little to chance and dislike surprises. They can also be uncomfortable in the face of change. In other words, they are inclined to be rule-bound. They often feel that they must attend personally to what goes on around them. This drive can be exceedingly strong, but its direction is to control what happens, not necessarily to achieve. They do achieve, but they want their achievement to be within the bounds of their personal control.

Highly aggressive individuals often believe that it is critical to be important. Accordingly, they strive for a position, both at work and in their private life, that implies that they are indeed significant people. They often drop names, and they make it clear that they can take care of things. They often develop a good deal of charisma. Their objective in life is to influence whatever circumstances in which they find themselves. They do not usually do the work themselves; rather, they influence others to do it. The aggressive is typically rather opinionated about what he feels he can influence. He is often an achiever because by completing a task, he can significantly increase his future span of control.

Aggressives are decisive and are risk takers. They are capable of performing as persuasive speakers and good motivators. They generally plan, organize, follow up, and control well. They delegate and then ensure that things will be completed.

The sensitized person can seem to some people to be a social wallflower, and so the assumption is that he possesses little or no drive; this assumption is mistaken. The sensitized person can be incredibly driven, but typically his aspirations and goals are highly internalized and obvious only to those who know him well. He works to the beat of his own drummer, and although generally poor at merchandizing his achievements, he is driven to succeed at tasks that he decides are worth the effort.

Because drive is such an inclusive characteristic, it can also be defined and may be better understood in terms of some joint behavior styles.

The overachiever-entrepreneur is distinguished from the others by the intensity and direction of his drive. This person derives an intrinsic satisfaction from the accomplishment itself. He knows what he is about and what is important to him. He is realistic in assessing what he can accomplish, but he consistently pushes ahead. The positively motivated person is a learner; he can influence and be influenced. He is motivated to get ahead because his need to accomplish is continuous, and he feels a need to be challenged. His desire to learn, to get better, and to excel focuses on his efforts. He addresses himself to results but attends to the means to the end also.

The active-passive individual is easy to live with since he virtually never causes difficulty through his behavior. He typically wants to be of help but is better at taking orders than at designing tasks for himself. Most people like him, although few would follow him as a leader. He looks to others for expectations. It is important to him that others think well of him. His motivation can be strong, but his purpose is to get along, avoid conflict, and be acceptable, not to achieve.

Active-passives limit their own growth potential by virtue of their objective in life. They are uncomfortable being in charge. They are often excellent number two persons. They are not decisive and have a low tolerance for risk. They are usually dependable and reliable but show little initiative. They are easily bothered by stress. How they feel about themselves is dependent upon how others feel about them.

Entrepreneur-aggressives are inclined to discount the importance of what other people think or wish. They tend to feel that their purposes and objectives are more important than those of others. They accept virtually no excuses for the failure of others to live up to the entrepreneur-aggressives' expectations. They are unconcerned about inconveniencing others if they will gain their own ends by doing so. Some achieve; some do not. Their purpose is not to achieve but rather to get their own way.

While entrepreneur-aggressives are hard taskmasters, it is also possible that they will inspire certain kinds of people to try harder than they might otherwise. They concern themselves only with getting the job done the way they want. They are not concerned with others except as sources of assistance. They do not develop others. They are highly decisive and often risk-oriented. They can be persuasive but not very adaptable. They delegate only tasks and follow up and control closely.

The interviewer should not try to label people according to the descriptions given above. These are given simply to stimulate your thinking in terms of styles or motivations. To determine an individual's motivation or drive level, you can explore numerous areas on the 120 Questionnaire and during the interview. A person's track record does not tell all, but, in general, a person who has achieved in the past will continue to achieve. Following are some indicators of drive.

Sports. Determine why he achieved and why it was important to him to achieve. Look for determination to excel, a commitment to excellence, initiative above expectations.

Extracurricular achievement positions. Altar server; Scout leader; sports team captain; honor society; class officer; student government leader; officer in hobby clubs or civic activities. Distinguish between participation and accomplishment in these areas. In and of themselves, none of the above denotes an achievement orientation, but they are clues; look for a pattern.

Employment. Determine what he has accomplished above the expectation for the job or the job description. (This question is good to use in reference checks.) Look for promotions within one company. Evaluate the competitiveness and achievement potential of the job itself; sales is usually more competitive than computer programming.

Military. A discharge rank or grade higher than usual, considering length of service, could be an indication of drive.

Academic. Grades in school could be an indication of drive. The following, however, should be considered when evaluating grades in school:

- The correlation between grade point average (GPA) and intelligence is not high.
- The correlation between GPA and later success is not high.
- The correlation between GPA and motivation to get good grades is high.
- School is typically a well-structured experience. Some people who are motivated to obtain good grades in school study, comply, and regurgitate information and thereby do well. Some of these people cannot do nearly as well in a nonacademic setting.
- Some do poorly in a very structured environment like school, particularly if at the time they view the degree requirements as not purposeful or related to their interests.

Aspirations. Achievers generally have a more well-defined set of aspirations. There usually exist a more well-defined plan and method to their efforts.

Personal characteristics of achievers.

1. *Energy.* If it is constructively directed, more energetic people tend to accomplish more.

2. *Competitiveness*. Achievers want to win and to be measured. Look for competitive activities.

3. *Independence*. Achievers typically learn to rely on themselves earlier. They are self-reliant and take responsibility for their own success or failure.

4. *Tenacity*. They get going when the going gets tough. They respond to a challenge rather than make excuses for failure or nonaction.

5. *Initiative*. They tend to make things happen rather than to react to what happens.

6. *Risk*. They are usually more willing to take risks.

7. *Desire to influence*. There is considerable evidence to indicate that the desire to influence, which derives from the power motive, results in a much more effective management style than does the achievement drive per se. The achiever will accomplish a lot, but the influencer will try to get others to achieve. Look for efforts on the part of the individual to get himself into a position of influence. The importance of the individual being in these positions is determined by why he is there and what he does in those positions, rather than just the fact that he achieved the positions.

Sense of pride. The achiever will typically give achievement-oriented responses (won contest; first in class; first in a race; won county tennis tournament) rather than note areas that might be personally satisfying but less achievement-oriented (proud of my family; graduated from college; was a Cub Scout; made $14,000).

Nature of work. Kind of work done or preferred indicates energy, which is a requirement for achievement. Hence, energy is indicated more by outside sales than by inside sales, by truck driving than by sorting mail, and by factory work than by bank work. Remember, these generalizations are not always true.

Response to, rewards of, work. More energy is indicated by action responses like doing, achieving, and solving than by responses like opportunity to learn, pleasant surroundings, or friendly associates.

Self-Esteem

Self-esteem is defined as confidence and a positive self-regard. People who have a high level of self-esteem demonstrate confidence and a positive self-regard. Self-esteem is considered to be a critical dimension in the assessment of potential. How a person views himself will impact on everything he does. It will impact on his use of his problem analysis skills, his decisiveness, his willingness to take risks, his motivation, his work standards, his adaptability, his reaction to stress, his relationships with people, and his aspirations.

Self-esteem is a feeling rather than an intellectual inventory of one's assets. In the eyes of others, one can be highly accomplished, famous, a champion, or a prized worker or craftsman and still have a crippling self-esteem. Self-esteem is not self-love in an egotistical sense. In fact, self-praise and boasting are classical symptoms of low self-esteem. If one truly accepts and appreciates his individual worth and importance, he has no need to boast or to try to impress others with his ability or possessions.

We are concerned here with the assessment of self-esteem. In many ways it is easier to describe low self-esteem or lack of confidence than its counterpart. One reason is that some people do a very good job of hiding how they feel about themselves. Some who lack confidence are withdrawn and timid while others are highly outgoing, assertive, and aggressive.

Those who have confidence accept themselves. They accept full responsibility for their behavior, for their successes and failures. They accept that they are not perfect, that they make mistakes, and that others may not feel as good about them as they feel about themselves. They are willing to permit others to disagree, to make mistakes, and to criticize them. They are able to separate what they do from what they are when they are criticized. They are able to separate the doer from the deed when criticizing others.

They feel neither a need always to have their own way nor a need always to permit others to have their own way. They are self-critical but not necessarily self-effacing. They are adaptable but not docile. They neither walk on others nor permit others to walk on them. They are optimistic about themselves and about others. In some ways, self-esteem is a measure of self-contentment. In essence, try to gauge how much the person actually believes the persona he is presenting to you and how much of his public image is just that—image.

This characteristic is difficult to gauge, even using the questions provided in the last chapter. The difficulty arises because it requires a significant amount of interpretation to distinguish the finer meanings of different responses to the questions; however, some guidelines are available.

True to form, the overachiever will candidly answer questions about his self-confidence. He is not afraid to admit that he is maturing and improving in this area. He may respond by describing situations when he was younger and emphasize that he would not act the same now. He may admit, for example, that he was stood up for a date at some point in his life but that at the time of the incident, he simply wondered if he misunderstood the time or place for the meeting. It would not occur to the overachiever that someone would simply not show up for an appointment without calling or somehow informing him. In retrospect, he might use the word *appointment* to describe a social date. The key ingredients of the overachiever's discussion of any failures he experienced will typically be in two areas. First, he will discuss the problem in a rational and logical manner, although it may deal with a personal issue. Second, he will almost always indicate that he learned something from the experience.

In sharp contrast to this logical problem analysis perspective on such a situation, the entrepreneur has difficulty admitting to flaws. In response to the direct question "Have you ever had any significant failures?", the entrepreneur is more likely than anyone else to respond, "No." Then if the entrepreneur is asked, "How about minor setbacks?" he will respond: "Well, yes, I guess so. Everyone has had some setbacks. Let me think for a second." Typically the entrepreneur is not so much ready to admit that he has failed at anything so much as he is beginning to feel the pressure that you want to hear about some problem he may have experienced. Remember, he is a very perceptive person, and he wants to be considered responsive to your questions. So he will admit to some setback that occurred to him at some point in his life. He may not feel that it was any real problem, but he will discuss it to please you, the interviewer.

The active will discuss such setbacks or any problematic issues openly and candidly. He will frequently respond: "Yes, I remember once I did something really stupid. I was only 18 at the time, but it was still dumb. I was with a bunch of my buddies, and we . . ." Again we see the group orientation and the willingness to open himself up emotionally to share some potentially semiserious event in his life.

The passive will grudgingly admit to having made some mistakes in his life, or in response to a polite question about "any regrets in your life so far," he may respond that he wishes he had taken more chances when he was younger. Passive people of all ages feel old and tend to blame their present circumstances and set of responsibilities for not being able to do more or risk more and therefore reach greater accomplishments than they currently have. Passives typically retort that they could be successful if they did not have stereo payments, car payments, mortgage payments, or X responsibilities.

It is easy to assume that the sensitized person has little self-esteem. He can be awkward socially and have some difficulty making small talk with people about issues of the day; however, although not boastful or outwardly conceited, he can be quite content. The sensitized person who does lack self-confidence can be cleverly sarcastic and biting in his remarks about others. Or he may imply that someone who has achieved some form of social notoriety was just lucky and did not deserve the acclaim he received. The sour grapes syndrome can be an indication of the sensitized person who does not feel self-confident.

The aggressive person can also appear to lack real self-confidence because he wants to be in charge of everything. He seeks out opportunities for social influence and control, and he typically sees greater opportunities to use his skills just at the next level above him. The fully confident aggressive person, however, is also able to stop and mix with people at all levels above and below his social level. He is not intimidated by his superiors, nor does he put himself above others. He may prefer a certain amount of pomp and circumstance, but he sees this as part of the inherent ritual of power, and he does not want to make others feel intimidated in his presence. He invites some criticism and debate of his ideas, but eventually he will expect his subordinates to close ranks and support his decisions.

The compulsive acts much like the overachiever in this regard. He simply responds to the questions in a rational and even-keeled manner. He may be noticeably non-plussed by the questions, but he will generally respond to them.

Following are indicators of self-esteem.

Attitudes toward self.

- High self-esteem: Neat appearance—personal and clothes. Competitive by choice, not need. Outgoing. Realist. Recognizes own strengths and shortcomings. Independent and self-reliant. Persistent. Feels free to express emotions.
- Low self-esteem: Sloppy appearance. Weak handshake. Overreacts to defeat. Withdrawn or timid. Perfectionist. Fails to recognize own shortcomings. Dependent. Insistent. Overly controlled or exaggerates emotions.

Attitudes toward others.

- High self-esteem: Meets gaze directly. Assertive. Participates in conversation. Recognizes others. Interest in others. Constructively criticizes others. Respects authority. Realistically trusting of others. Feels equal to others. Easily meets new people. Listens to others. Easily accepts compliments or praise.
- Low self-esteem: Unwillingness to look another person in the eye. Aggressive or domineering. Dominates conversation; compulsive talker. Insensitive to others. Confirmed people pleaser or name dropper. Cannot pass up an opportunity to straighten others out. Resents authority. Distrusting of others or overly trusting. Feels superior or inferior to others. Timid or aggressive with new people. Defers to others. Embarrassed by praise or seeks praise all the time. Jealous, envious, or suspicious.

Work characteristics.

- High self-esteem: Comfortable in new situations. Admits mistakes. Objectively evaluates himself and his performance. Achieves and wants to do well. Willing to take risks. Decisive. Persuasive. Learns from his mistakes. Meets challenge with quiet confidence. Meets conflict realistically.
- Low self-esteem: Tense, anxious, nervous. Covers mistakes or is defeated by them. Prideful, boasting, or underestimates his ability. Aching need for money, power, or prestige. Will avoid risk. Indecisive or overly decisive. Adamant. Defeated by his mistakes. Resents challenge or overestimates ability to handle it. Avoids or creates conflict.

Self-Development

A person who has a self-development orientation makes an active effort to improve himself and to acquire knowledge and skills. This dimension can be difficult to assess, but it is critical to the assessment of potential. The person who wants to learn, grow, improve, or get better, other things being equal, will make a superior employee or manager compared with the person who considers himself to be a finished product. A person is not going to be able to significantly learn, grow, improve, or get better unless he recognizes his strengths and shortcomings, has a desire to grow, commits himself to growing, and does so.

To assess one's orientation toward development, we need to know what the individual understands about himself. Look at the 120 Questionnaire, especially those areas where the individual is asked to list his strengths, shortcomings, criticisms he has received, and actions he has taken to correct these criticisms.

People who want to grow open themselves to many sources of input. They learn from their own mistakes and from the mistakes of others. They accept criticism. They strive to raise their standards for their own performance. They are willing and able to evaluate their own performance. They are willing to admit they do not know something and to ask for help. They are willing to discuss their mistakes and typically have taken action to see that they do not repeat them. They are learners. Typically they have taken courses or involved themselves in activities for the purpose of improving themselves personally.

When reviewing the 120 Questionnaire, note whether the person was willing to respond to the key questions noted above and then whether he was willing to be open and frank or just superficial. If he indicates he has received no criticism, ask if he deserved any or if his boss criticized others. Ask him to evaluate his current job performance, school performance, or military performance. Note whether the picture he presents is balanced, objective, and thorough or superficial and highly biased. Note his response to criticism given by others in the past. Ask if there are ways in which he might have performed better in various areas of his experience.

The responses of the seven traits to this set of questions are similar to the responses for the questions on self-esteem, which should be reviewed for additional understanding.

Listed below are some indications of self-development orientation.

School. Chose elective courses for purposeful development.

Spare time activities. Reads for the purpose of technical or personal development. Goes to night school and takes courses, especially when not working on a basic degree. Has taken courses for adults like English composition, speech, Dale Carnegie. These become even more significant when the person has recognized a shortcoming and has taken courses on his own initiative.

Self-evaluation. The individual talks about learning, growing, and improving rather than about how good he is, indicating that he feels he is a finished product.

Other people. When he talks about others he respects, he talks about them in terms of learning and growing rather than being finished products.

Strengths and shortcomings. Subject is willing to discuss shortcomings. He discusses both in specific terms; for example, "good problem solver" or "have trouble making decisions" is more specific than "reliable" or "sometimes procrastinate."

Actions taken to correct criticisms. Indicates specific actions to correct areas of deficiency; for example, "took Kepner-Tregoe course" or "began to carefully consider all sides of the issue" versus "tried to get better" when criticized for poor problem analysis skills.

Reward of jobs. Subject mentions specifics in terms of learning, opportunity to grow, emphasis on training, or development of skills.

Stress Tolerance

Stress tolerance is defined as the ability to function in a controlled, effective manner under stress. Obviously, the first problem in assessing stress tolerance is to determine whether the interviewee is under stress. For most people, an interview or evaluation situation is itself stressful. If there are no visible signs of stress, we will have to assume that the interviewee is comfortable or at least is able to handle the situation in a controlled and effective manner. In general, it is not a good idea to attempt to conduct a stress interview. The interview will ordinarily be more productive for both parties if the candidate is relaxed and participative. The interviewer can, however, in a nonthreatening manner, disagree with a concept or idea the individual puts forth, or the interviewer can purposefully misinterpret something the individual has said. Some will feel stress in this situation; some will not. The interviewer, however, has an opportunity to observe how the interviewee thinks on his feet and how he deals with what he may consider to be criticism.

In general, those who possess higher levels of self-esteem are less likely to perceive a situation as being stressful or at least are more likely to function in a controlled, effective manner under stress. Review the indicators of self-esteem. Those who meet new people easily and are comfortable in new situations are less likely to feel stress in an interview. Those who meet challenge with quiet confidence and who meet conflict realistically are less likely to feel stress or can handle it. Some individuals will be visibly nervous to the extent that their nervousness will negatively impact on their performance. There are a number of reasons, all related to problems of self-esteem. Under perceived pressure, the traits will become more themselves; under perceived intense pressure, their mannerisms can become exaggerated. Consider the following.

The overachiever can become flustered and stressed. Under these circumstances he is likely to demonstrate increasingly rigid behavior and appear more mechanical. He may have difficulty demonstrating much emotion beyond some obviously rehearsed warmth and polite social interaction. He will rely more on the apparent use of logic and rationality to explain his answers without appropriate commentary to explain himself more fully.

Under intense pressure the entrepreneur will work at demonstrating extra smoothness and gentle charm. His movements may be exaggerated, and his manner may become slightly affected. He becomes a caricature of his own worst image—a person faking social comfort when he really does not feel the composure he is so desperately trying to convey.

The active person will typically become more animated and socially excited. He may stand up and begin to walk around with the explanation that he has been sitting all morning and that he needs a break.

Passives are concerned with doing well. They perceive the interview as an evaluation, and they are unsure of their ability to measure up. Their exaggerated concern with doing well creates stress and a less effective performance.

The sensitized are simply uncertain in any new situation, even if expectations are well defined. They will often be reticent and noncommunicative. On the other hand, some aggressive individuals handle the situation by being assertive and otherwise coming on strong. This distinction can be determined by carefully assessing the dimension of self-esteem. Finally, highly aggressive people have an exaggerated need to control the circumstances in which they find themselves. In an interview, they are not in control, and some will try to control the interview and thereby display their response to stress while some will openly display their resentment about being interviewed.

Adaptability

This dimension is defined as the ability to adjust one's approach to reach a goal and to adapt to varied environments. Adaptability, decisiveness, and risk taking are the three dimensions where more is not necessarily better. In other words, it is possible to be too decisive, too risky, and too adaptable. One needs to be able and willing to adapt sufficiently so as to be able to effect a compromise or otherwise get the job done, but not so adaptable that he becomes a Casper Milquetoast.

A person who can adjust his approach is sensitive to a number of factors in a given situation:

- significance of the problem
- urgency required
- his position, authority, and influence
- the needs of others involved

He understands give-and-take, compromise, and fair play. He is results-oriented. He is able to keep his eye on the objective and to shift gears when things get off-track.

A person who can adapt to varied environments is more easily able to get into new situations and handle them effectively. He is resourceful and can apply his knowledge and experience to new situations. He sees the positive aspects of change. He can be successful in a number of different positions (other things being equal) because he can adapt to new conditions or requirements.

People who have a positive self-regard and above-average initiative often display adaptability. Their confidence permits them to deal effectively with new and different situations, challenges, and varied environments, and, because of their initiative, they are practiced in doing the same. (Caution: high levels of apparently purposeless or unfocused adaptability may indicate low self-esteem and low initiative.) Also, note the person's adaptability to criticisms received; action taken would be a good clue.

The 120 Questionnaire can provide a few tentative clues to a person's adaptability or lack of it, for example, participation in multiple sports or several different extracurricular activities. Also, several hobbies or success in two or three different kinds of jobs could be clues to his adaptability. Look at how the person has made various decisions and how he handles stress.

During the interview, note how he adapts to you, to the flow and pace of the conversation, and to the shifts from fact to opinion or from technical to personal topics. Check with others who may interview him and note whether he can adapt to different individuals or styles of interviewing.

The overachiever can and will show various degrees of adaptability. As a general rule, he prefers to maintain a fairly simple, uncomplicated, but self-described logical pattern of social behavior. He prefers what others might describe as a somewhat dull routine to exciting possibilities of quick change; however, under intense pressure he can and will adapt quickly to a changed set of circumstances. For example, the unexpected death of a parent during teenage years will not necessarily interrupt his college education, or the sudden loss of employment due to no fault of his own will not deter him from immediately looking for a new position while maintaining a positive emotional outlook. So while on the surface he may appear to lack significant skills in this area, when the pressure is on, he will adapt quite quickly and generally do quite well.

The entrepreneur will typically describe himself as incredibly adaptable and flexible. Part of his self-image and beliefs is that he can handle extreme amounts of pressure without showing significant strain; in some ways, he is right. He can appear to handle the pressure, but in reality he typically changes environments and avoids any buildup of pressure. For example, rather than stick with the pressures of a given project in a job, he will frequently quit the job and find new employment. His work record will be a history of one-, two- or three-year stints with different companies. He will invariably have a good reason for his changes, like "They lied to me," "Companywide cutbacks," "Sales territory went dry," "I wanted to move out West," or "I had a better offer." Each of these reasons can be interpreted as adequate for changing; however, a long pattern of short employment stops (for example, more than four jobs in the eight years after school has been completed) can indicate a lack of ability to respond to pressure and an inability to adapt to changing circumstances.

Typically the active almost by definition is highly adaptable and flexible. He sees change as a necessary part of life and is proud to be part of it. The overachiever-active person will respond to the need for a change in work with a comment like: "I like that idea, it appeals to me a lot, and you know me I'm usually ready for almost anything. But let me make sure that I understand the opportunity you are describing."

The passive person has a difficult time accepting change and hence is not highly adaptable. He prefers the tried-and-true manner of doing business. The occasionally heard response to a question about change is: "Well, I don't really know about that [the process for solving the problem]. Around here, we have always done it this way. I don't see any real reason to change from doing it this way, and I plan always to do it this way. So, I guess we won't be needing your new ideas." Refusing a corporate promotion that requires a physical move can indicate a lack of adaptability and flexibility, even though such refusal may be couched in terms of a spouse's refusal to move, the need for children to remain in one certain school, and so on.

The sensitized person can appear to be uniquely adaptable and flexible but at the same time incredibly stubborn and fixed. Generally, the sensitized person requires little special attention and is pleased to be left alone to complete his work in a professional manner. He can also, however, become very attached to what others might describe as peculiar habits or idiosyncrasies. For example, he may be willing to revamp and revise an entire project at short notice and with minimal assistance from anyone else, but he will also insist on reading the newspaper in his office the first 20 minutes of his workday. This insistence may cause him to be fired, an action that he will commonly accept because reading the newspaper is very important to him. He will accept being terminated rather than stop reading the paper.

The aggressive person prefers to avoid change, unless he is in charge of the new activity. The more socially mature aggressive sees change as inevitable and frequently plans his day around making sure that he is still leading the operation, department, or company after the change has taken place. The aggressive is not so much concerned with change per se, but he is very focused on the outcome of the change and how it will affect his position, authority, and overall responsibility in the work unit. He does not want to lose any control as a result of the change and generally expects to gain some additional control.

The compulsive person is little affected by change. He generally adapts quickly and effectively as long as his workplace is in order and he is allowed to return to his projects in a reasonable period of time with few interruptions. He is oriented toward work achievement for its own sake. As long as his immediate tasks are unchanged, he will adapt quickly. If the tasks are changed, he needs to be given a new set of priorities and goals.

Persuasiveness

Persuasiveness is defined as effectiveness in leading others to a desired course of action. The dimension is obviously closely tied to communication. It is possible, however, to lead others or perhaps to push others to desired courses of action and not be an effective transmitter of facts and ideas (communicator). This concept points up the emotional, enthusiastic, and motivational aspect of persuasiveness.

Persuasiveness, however, is much more than emotion or enthusiasm. In fact, some effective persuaders or influencers can accomplish their purposes with little or no display of emotion or enthusiasm. In the process of assessing the dimension of persuasiveness, the interviewer must first and foremost be attentive to the result. Did he persuade? Did he lead others to his point of view? Did he get the job done? It is easy to be caught up in the means of persuasion, but the effectiveness quality can be assessed only in terms of results.

The overachiever has well-developed problem analysis skills. He thinks in a very orderly and logical manner. He is careful to think through his point of view and to consider alternatives. He is a careful decision maker. He is well organized in his preparation and presentation. His communication is typically concise and precise. He is controlled in his actions and speech. He never raises his voice or displays emotion or enthusiasm. He has confidence in his point of view and expects the logic of his point of view to speak for itself. He feels that what he says is sufficient and that he should not have to sell himself. If his argument meets resistance, he either repeats his logic or, in the same controlled manner, points out the errors in the logic of his adversary.

The entrepreneur is frequently highly persuasive. He reads people quickly and effectively. At the same time, he can modify his presentation to fit his perception of the needs of his audience. So he will readily and strategically endorse whatever he thinks a client wants to hear so that he will purchase a product. He is clever at making black look gray and gray, white. He can readily give examples of where he sold someone of an idea. Then he will almost laugh with pride over the fact that the person really did not necessarily need or want the product. He is proud of his ability to "play the game," and he generally sees himself coming out ahead in the process. He can, however, be a short-term player and may be caught up in the euphoria of his immediate and potentially short-range success; that is, he can have some difficulty maintaining a long-term relationship with his clients.

The active person, almost by definition, has the potential to be highly persuasive. He is genuinely people-oriented and projects a natural sense of enthusiasm for his activities. He is readily likable and finds pleasure in social interaction. His actual degree of persuasiveness may, in part, depend upon how much overachiever is also in his temperament.

The overachiever-active can, of course, be logical, thorough, well prepared, and organized in his presentation and efforts to persuade. On the other hand, he may not be any of these. He is confident of his ability to deal with people. He is more personal, more the influencer. He is not dependent on logic, his position, or his authority. He is able to express his emotions. He is generally sensitive to the reactions of others. He will typically display a higher level of adaptability than will the logical persuader. He is a better motivator. He is quick on his feet and can effectively handle conflict. He is usually more verbose than the logical persuader, and his communication is more colorful than precise. If his argument meets resistance, he will try another tack. He has multiple techniques; he can be either demanding or giving, impatient or tolerant, adamant or conciliatory.

The passive person typically is not highly persuasive. He can be somewhat negative in outlook and pessimistic in approach to problem solving so he can throw a damper on someone else's persuasive presentation. The passive who acts in this way, however, can also fill the role of "quality-control checker"; that is, he will slow down any runaway enthusiasm for an idea and make sure that the underlying assumptions are checked and verified before everyone wholeheartedly endorses the idea. In this sense, the passive person can play an important devil's advocate role to a group-think process.

The aggressive person is also capable of being naturally persuasive. By definition he seeks positions of social power and control. If he also possesses a solid amount of the overachiever or active traits, then he can be a highly team-oriented and persuasive person. He may insist on being in charge of the group activity, but he will be well prepared for presentations and will act in a self-confident, controlled, and charismatic fashion. Where the entrepreneur reads individuals especially well, the aggressive person apparently possesses an intuitive feel for the crowd. He knows how to use pauses in his speech pattern for dramatic effect and crowd-pleasing results.

Just because a person is not one of the typically persuasive types does not mean that he cannot have a commanding presence when facing a group. It is important to consider how some other behavior styles can also be highly persuasive. For example, the overachiever-sensitized person is neither as rigid or controlled as the logical persuader, nor is he as emotional or flamboyant as the personal persuader. It is easy to underestimate his persuasive skills because he is typically unassuming and highly selective about when, where, and on what issues he will assert his point of view. He is generally confident of his point of view, but he does not set out to sell, persuade, or convince anybody of anything until he feels it is important to do so. He is just as selective when it comes to others' influencing him. He is a good listener and open to being influenced, but the closer the persuader gets to his commit-ment, the more personal resolve and selectivity will the quietly confident one display.

The overachiever-sensitized person, typically, is a more mature individual and often has a more well-defined value system. He can describe what is important to him. If your value system differs from his and you try to lead him to your point of view, he will respect it, but will be most affirmative, unwavering, and calmly resistant to your efforts. His values are firmly held and rarely compromised.

When he decides that an issue is important and that he needs to persuade others, he begins with a soft sell. In fact, he begins long before the current issue by establishing a constructive environment and management style based on respect. If he meets resistance, he will try to determine why and will attempt to reason with the individual involved. If this attempt fails, he can become insistent while still being sensitive to the other person. If the issue is important (relatively) and all else fails, he will become autocratic.

Communication

Communication is defined as the ability to transmit facts and ideas effec-tively. Since an interview is dependent upon communication, one would think that this would be an easy dimension to evaluate. Many interviewers, however, are so caught up in the content of what is said or written that they pay little attention to how it is said or written. People communicate in different ways. There is more to be learned than whether a person is a good or bad communicator. One person may be quick on his feet and hence able to respond quickly and appropriately in an interview. Another may be slow but careful and selective in how he responds. Both can be effective in trans-mitting facts and ideas.

Some may be poor verbal communicators but are able to express them-selves effectively in writing; the reverse may also be true. Some are consider-ably better able to communicate facts than ideas. Some find it easy to talk about things, processes, or procedures but find it difficult to discuss con-cepts. Some are precise and to the point, while others ramble on intermi-nably.

It is not necessary to ask specific questions to assess communication skills during the interview, but many observations can be made. A person's ability to communicate effectively is the result of intelligence and personality traits. The overachiever can be matter-of-fact and somewhat dry but generally is quite organized and complete in stating his response to any variety of ques-tions. The entrepreneur is frequently glib, clever, and somewhat smooth in presenting his material. He can make a very positive first impression, but he may be simply parroting information he has memorized for a standard interview, so ask him some thinking questions and gauge his response.

The active is frequently quite animated, outgoing, cheerful, and emotionally positive with people so that he can interact with almost anybody and create a people-oriented and positive impression. The passive person can be slow and methodical and need some reassurance to be effective about stating his strengths. In a similar way the sensitized person is frequently introverted, and although he is often creative and insightful, verbal communication can scare him; he especially needs understanding and reassurance. On the contrary, the aggressive can appear to be quite an authority on a variety of subjects.

Review the 120 Questionnaire and note how the individual has communicated facts and ideas. Note especially those items where he is asked to describe situations. Also look for complete answers, which are concise and clear.

During the interview

1. Does he address himself directly to questions?
2. Does he get to the point or ramble on?
3. Is he able to describe concepts and people, as well as facts and things?
4. Does he maintain a logical sequence when describing procedures or chronological events?
5. Does he talk too much or not enough?
6. Does he listen?
7. Does he use professional jargon?
8. What is his level of vocabulary?
9. Are there any personal quirks that detract from his communication?

Interview Interpretation

This chapter is designed to help the interviewer bring together some of the separate threads that have been introduced throughout the book. The interviewer is being invited to summarize, analyze, and interpret all the data that have been collected in the interview process. At first reading, this process may sound awesome; however, if the interview process has been conducted properly, interpretation should merely be the next step in the sequence leading to a final decision and be no more or less difficult than the steps that preceded it.

You should learn three primary ideas from this chapter. The first two are technical and can be mastered with basic learning techniques; the third may take more time. The ideas are

1. Study the processes and concepts the previous chapters have introduced and described. Begin to think in terms of typing people. Specifically, use the seven basic behavior traits and the multiple behavior styles to analyze and categorize people. Not every individual you know or meet will conveniently fit into one of the behavior traits, but most people can be approximately summarized by using these traits.

2. Review the 120 and 220 questionnaires so that you are familiar with their content and understand how differing responses to the various questions can help you begin to categorize individuals into the traits and behavior styles.

3. Learn to trust your own judgment in terms of recognizing behavior patterns and categorizing individuals into certain behavior traits. The learning process will take time and experience, but as you use the system you will become increasingly comfortable and accurate doing so.

The chapter begins with the honest caveat that the interview interpretation process is both science and art; that is, successful interviewing is based on factual review and intuitive processes. The chapter reviews some basic rules of evidence for evaluating a candidate and concludes with some suggestions for forms that are useful when making notes on the suitability of a given individual.

The chapter examines a condensed but real interview situation. This example starts by reminding the interviewer of the importance of reviewing and understanding the job description. The chapter then repeats some of the steps first mentioned in chapter 4 about preparing for the interview. It then examines these steps with a new example and more information.

OVERVIEW

Before we begin to evaluate the information we have gathered, we must understand the art of interpretation. When interpreting data, we are forced to draw conclusions and summarize and categorize information until it fits into our parameters. This process has little to do with our evaluation of a given candidate; it serves only to help the interviewer present, at a later date, what he has discovered.

Interpretation is really the art of enhancing facts with information you have determined by other means. Most of this book has endeavored to impart to the reader some kind of scientific approach to the interview process, but this is useless without an interviewer who can glean the true meaning from apparent truths offered by the candidate.

To begin the interpretation stage of the evaluation process, the interviewer must put aside all information, evidence, attributes, and behaviors and answer some basic questions. Without being influenced by the constraints of the behavior traits, form a mental picture of the individual. At this point, you have a definite impression of the individual and have drawn conclusions about his abilities. Right now, these conclusions can be taken with a grain of salt until they are proven by evidence and categorized.

The interviewer must ask himself some questions to form an initial impression of the candidate. Consider your feelings about the candidate as a person and, for purposes of this discussion, consider the last candidate you interviewed for a position with the company. Did anything about the candidate just interviewed that is not directly related to the position influence your impressions of him? If you are being honest with yourself, you will almost have to answer this question yes. Why? Because a number of ancillary factors can interfere with the interviewing process. For example, as part of the ongoing research into the process of interviewing, over 500 individuals who regularly interview for employment positions were asked a series of questions about their interviewing practices. Listed below are the questions we asked them and the percent of respondents who answered yes to the questions. Remember, these are professional interviewers.

Question	Percent
1. Are you more impressed with candidates who ask many questions?	82
2. Do you give equal consideration to someone who has been fired from his last position?	37

3. Are you more impressed with someone who is overconfident than with the person who is shy? 64
4. Does the physical attractiveness of a given candidate influence your hiring recommendation? 67
5. Are you more interested in intelligence than in the social style of the candidate? 82
6. Are you more impressed if the candidate looks you in the eye for a good part of the interview? 73
7. Does it matter what college the candidate attended? 81
8. Do you make a solid recommendation based on a first impression of the candidate? 65
9. Is apparent enthusiasm an especially important trait? 87
10. Is apparent ambition an especially important trait? 96

As the results of this survey show, we all have biases and predispositions that will affect our judgment in the interview process. It is important, however, to try to be aware of them and understand that we are being influenced by factors that are not necessarily job-related. By being aware of these factors, we can become better interviewers.

RULES OF INTERPRETATION

Now you are ready to test your impressions against the evidence you have gathered; you will take a good look at all the information available to you and revise your conclusions. There are some rules to be followed here. The interviewer must respect the fact that he has a responsibility to his company and to the candidate to take his job seriously. His decision will have repercussions in the candidate's life as well as in the future of the company. The interviewer must decide from this moment whether his intention is to hire someone to fill a position or someone to take part in a growing, changing, successful company.

The interviewer must have confidence in his ability to make a responsible and correct decision. He must have confidence in his ability as a student of human behavior and as an interviewer. A lack of confidence will result in a poor performance, as the interviewer well knows after studying this book. Confidence will come only with practice and a thorough knowledge of the material covered here.

The importance of understanding the demands of the position for which you are hiring cannot be stressed enough. Keep skills and attributes in perspective, explore their long-range effects, and remember that you may want the individual eventually to be able to take on more responsibility.

More than the above, the interviewer must know what he is looking for before the interview. If one does not know this, then it becomes impossible to direct the interview toward obtaining any particular information. You will also be unable to follow up on any potentially useful information if you do not know what would be useful. Keep the individual in front of you until you have a thorough understanding of him as well as his responses to your questions.

All of the processes explained here are only a means to the end of understanding human behavior and, in particular, the candidate's behavior. If you truly understand the person, interpreting the information you have gathered will be much easier. Do not concentrate on the act of documenting, categorizing, and rating as much as you concentrate on the individual. The individual and all his idiosyncrasies are more important than the rating system, with all of its accuracy.

RULES OF EVIDENCE

1. *Be objective.* Know your values and yourself and know that these things affect your objectivity. Controlling the interview will allow you to keep your objective distance. You will not be drawn in by an interesting, outgoing individual if you keep him on track and continue to extract the information that you think is necessary. Give extra effort to ensuring objectivity when you run into such a person in an interview situation.

2. *Keep your observations in perspective.* Not all of the evidence you gather is of tantamount importance. Some facts will be more useful than others. Here are some helpful ways to decide.

3. *Fact is better than conjecture.* If an individual has proven results as a manager, they are more valuable than his feeling that he would be a successful manager. Both must be considered in the context of his responses to the managerial skills questions.

4. *Your observations are more valuable than his reported observations.* If you observed in him some quality that you think is valuable, then this observation is more reliable than his report that he has this quality. Also your observation is more valuable than the fact that he held a position where he would normally have to use this skill.

5. *More evidence leads to more accurate conclusions.* If you notice a quality once in an interview, it is not of much consequence as evidence, but if you noted it a few times, then you can assume your conclusion will be accurate. Also if a number of areas in the individual's life show a drive to achieve, this information is more valuable than information that he has achieved only in one area.

6. *The most recent information is the best.* Remember that people change and learn. An individual who was not a risk taker as a young person may well have grown in confidence and adventurousness since then. In the same light, a person who has never exhibited a quality historically is not likely to learn it after you hire him.

7. *Pay more attention to the individual's attitude than to the content of his remarks.* His words may say one thing, but his responses to your questions will be much more revealing of his attitudes toward himself, others, and his environment.

Chart 7.1
Position Analysis Chart—Generic Sales Manager

	Low	Medium	High
	- - - - - - - - -	5	+ + + + + + +
Overachiever	/////////////////////////////		
Entrepreneur	//////////////////		
Active	///////////////////////////////////		
Passive	////////////		
Sensitized	////////		
Aggressive	//		
Compulsive	////////////////		

AN EXAMPLE

Step 1: Review the SKAP Analysis

Chapter 4 provides a brief summary of the steps involved in conducting a SKAP analysis of a given position. This brief review was not intended to be complete or even adequate for analyzing a position; however, it did review some of the critical steps in the process. Moreover, chapter 4 includes a chart for defining the behavior traits included in a generic sales position. This chart defined the position in terms of the seven behavior traits. It can be used again to define graphically the type and level of traits that might be useful for a generic sales management position in a given company.

Chart 7.1, the Position Analysis Chart, has been completed for the generic sales manager. Take a pencil and mark your own impressions for the level of each of the seven traits discussed in chapter 2 that you think a generic sales management position requires. This process will help you keep clear in your mind the relationship between the position requirements SKAP profile and the interpersonal skills of the candidate being interviewed.

Chart 7.1 suggests that a candidate with an overachiever-active-aggressive behavior style will be a good interpersonal fit for the sales management position. Generally such a person will be disciplined, controlled, energetic, and interpersonally outgoing but also socially aggressive, eager to be a team leader, and, to some degree, eager to control and influence group activities.

A person with a reasonable or average but not necessarily high entrepreneur trait is preferred because the position is salary-based with some bonus for group production and requires a person to build a sales team. Thus money motivation should be part of the candidate's trait pattern but not the dominant trait. The passive and sensitized traits are low because the position requires a high degree of interpersonal contact and the ability socially and charismatically to lead others to achieve group goals. The compulsive trait is ranked average because, although details per se are of contributory importance in the position, they are not critical.

The levels of entrepreneur and compulsive traits have the most flexibility in this description. The candidate can be either higher or lower than described, and this variation will have little effect on the overall appropriateness of the candidate. The other traits, however, should have about the level described.

This description of the interpersonal skill set for the candidate does not mean that candidates with other levels of interpersonal skills will automatically be rejected. As a preliminary analysis of the position, however, the chart does provide an outline for the type of interpersonal skills that should be able do the job well. The emphasis is on the importance of higher scores on the three factors of overachiever, active, and aggressive and lower scores on the sensitized and passive traits, with average or a wide variation around average for the entrepreneur and compulsive traits.

Now let's review additional information about this position and some information about a given candidate. This information represents a condensed version of information typically available about a candidate.

Step 2: Examine Related Written Material

To understand the candidate better, let's review the following three items: (1) position fact sheet (information on the position), (2) candidate resume (including the cover letter), and (3) candidate responses to the 120 Questionnaire.

POSITION FACT SHEET

Job Title: Sales Manager (food items)
SKAP Analysis: College degree or equivalent work experience.
Position requires supervising a field sales/service force of 7–10 individuals who are college-educated adults, have 1–3 years' work experience, and can influence but not entirely control the results they achieve.

Some (2–5 years) selling experience.
Position requires knowledge of selling techniques and methods. Should have completed sales training course(s) and generally be aware of methods of presenting features, benefits, and advantages of a given product.

Some (2–7 years) sales management experience, preferably with a major food organization (e.g., Pepsi, Coke, P&G, Nabisco).

Works independently.

Minimal supervision. Will be given monthly and quarterly sales goals but expected to reach goals by motivating, leading, and inspiring sales force members.

Motivated by salary with opportunity for 20–30 percent yearly bonus.

Compensation package includes base and bonus based on results of sales unit sales, not individual sales.

Socially persuasive.

Must be able to motivate, inspire, and lead a professional but relatively inexperienced sales force to achieve increasingly higher goals.

Highly energetic.

Some Saturday meetings and overnight (weekend) travel may be required. Must possess the energy to do this.

Some knowledge of food store operations, retail sales, and food products helpful but not mandatory.

Setting: Today's date: December 1, 1989

Location: Philadelphia, PA

Salary range: Base $40,000–$50,000; Bonus of up to additional $10,000–$15,000.

RESUME

John Block
115 Hidden Valley Road
Radnor, PA 17890
(215) 473-1211

Objective

I am an educated, disciplined, organized individual who is interested in demonstrating my skills as a sales manager. I have a short but generally successful history of leading people and feel I can be successful with your organization.

Work History

Frito-Lay, Philadelphia, PA
Senior sales representative
9-88—current

Calling on grocery store headquarter accounts to sell our food programs at chain-wide level. Increased market penetration 20 percent each year and showed dramatic improvement on customer satisfaction index.

Frito-Lay, Philadelphia, PA
Sales representative
7-84—7-88

Calling on grocery store accounts and selling our products at differently sized stores. Initially I was assigned a territory that was ranked eighth out of nine territories. After three years the territory was ranked second, and in my last year territory was ranked first. Left this position for a promotion to senior sales representative as described above.

U.S. Navy
Lieutenant (jg)
7-80—6-84

Naval officer assigned to battleship duty (one year) and basic training officer in San Diego, CA. Achieved Outstanding Leadership Award for developing training activities.

Education

University of Michigan, Ann Arbor, MI
9-76—6-80 B.S., marketing
GPA: 3.2
ROTC scholarship

Cover Letter

John Block
115 Hidden Valley Road
Radnor, PA 17890
(215) 473-1211

Box 123
Philadelphia Inquirer
Philadelphia, PA

Dear Sir/Madam:

This letter is in response to your advertisement in the Sunday edition of the *Philadelphia Inquirer* under the heading "Field Sales Manager—Food Industry."

My resume is enclosed for your review. As you can see, I have the sales representative experience your ad describes, and I think I have the management experience your ad describes, but not in a sales capacity.

My sales representative experience is very similar to the requirements stated in the ad. I have been very successful in sales because I am organized, hardworking, and achievement-oriented. In the sales process I am diplomatically polite but sometimes have difficulty accepting the first "no" as a final answer.

My management experience stems from two primary sources. In college I held two fraternity positions, pledge trainer and president. During my four years in the military I gained considerable management experience. As a military officer I was able to inspire and lead a group of young recruits as well as motivate and, if appropriate, push the more mature personnel under my command to achieve our unit objectives. I was commended for this skill by the base commander.

If you see sufficient match between my education, skills, and background and your needs, please contact me at your earliest convenience.

Yours truly,

John Block

JB/hp

Candidate Responses to the 120 Questionnaire

120 Q: Describe your development. What factors (family, education, work, etc.) influenced you to be the person that you are today?

120 A: My family had the most influence on my growing up. I learned to listen, anticipate, and effectively communicate my thoughts and feelings. It became apparent to me fairly early on that the kids who got in trouble either were looking for attention or didn't have a plan to achieve their goals. I have always been very goal-oriented. Early on, I believed that hard work and luck lead to success. Now I understand that successful people make their own luck. My parents generally supported me, and although they were always there if I needed them, they encouraged me not to need them.

120 Q: Did you interrupt or fail to finish any level of your education? If so, please explain.

120 A: No, I completed every program that I started. Finishing what I start has become very important to me.

120 Q: What kind of work would you enjoy doing 5 years from now? How much would you want to earn then?

120 A: This is a difficult question to answer. To me, right now, five years seems like a long time. Long-term (I suppose this is what you are really asking), I would like to be the vice president of sales of a major organization. I think of sales management as a position of great leverage, where a person can influence people and events far beyond what he can do as an individual sales representative. Anyway, in five years I would say an income of between $75 and $100K.

120 Q: As a youngster did anyone inspire you to achieve your goals? Who, what did they do?

120 A: Sports heroes have always been my greatest role models. I have average-plus athletic ability, but I always marvel at the skill and grace of some of the greats of any athletic contest. I guess Jim Thorpe is my all-time hero.

120 Q: I feel that money

120 A: is a way of keeping score and therefore important, but not the number one criterion of success.

120 Q: Working on fine points

120 A: is something I hate, but I do it, and I check and double-check.

Step 3: Make Note of Questions About Any Incomplete, Curious, or Confusing Items

In the example of John Block not many responses seem to fit this category. A quick review of his history indicates that he completed college on ROTC scholarship, completed his military obligation, has evidently successfully sold at an entry level for years, and now seems to have been successful at a higher level of selling. Clearly he lacks the sales management experience requirement, but he may possess the raw talents to be effective in this role even without the stated experience. He seems to be worth the additional time for an interview.

Step 4: Organize and Record Your Initial Impressions

Use the Candidate Analysis Chart (Chart 7.2) to chart your impressions from the information you have. These are preliminary ideas, subject to modification upon further exploration during the interview. Review the position, the candidate fact sheet, candidate resume, and candidate sample responses to the 120 Questionnaire. Can you draw any tentative conclusions from them? Can you identify any topic areas that need additional exploration in the interview? Do you have some (even vague) impressions of the candidate? To the extent possible, using the information above, fill in the Candidate Analysis Chart for Mr. John Block.

So far, Mr. Block seems to possess a high degree of the overachiever and aggressive traits. He also seems to possess an average plus amount of the active energy and some sense of team spirit, but his actual degree of interpersonal warmth may need to be carefully investigated.

He seems competitive, and so the entrepreneurial trait is marked average, and he is reasonably detail-minded and systematic but generally concerned with achieving his goals for the sake of accomplishment. This information suggests that the compulsive trait is in the average range, perhaps higher. So far, we would probably place his sensitized and passive traits as average minus, with the possibility of placing them even lower after meeting him.

The key question becomes, Can he build a successful unit? Or is the apparent sales success he has achieved dependent upon his individual ability? Moreover, can he achieve goals through others? In essence, the question becomes, Is he a star passing in the night, or can he develop, build, and maintain a sales force of people who can learn to operate in the same

Chart 7.2
Candidate Analysis Chart—John Block

	Low	Medium	High	
	– – – – – – – –	5	+ + + + + + +	
Overachiever	////////////////////			
Entrepreneur	////////////			
Active	////////			
Passive	//			
Sensitized	//			
Aggressive	/////////////////////			
Compulsive	//////////			

manner as he apparently does? The answer to these questions will depend on how he conducts himself during the interview.

Chapter 6 introduced and defined 13 additional characteristics, which are frequently included in an evaluation of a candidate for a position requiring some degree of interpersonal skill. The candidate's responses to questions about these topics can be used to define his behavior style. Chart 6.1 can be used as a convenient summary form for rating the person and these topics and defining him in terms of the seven behavior traits. It can also be used to document information he provides during the interview to define his level of interpersonal skill.

So that you can gain familiarity with the chart, some of the nonverbal impressions and verbal responses Mr. John Block provided during the interview will be reviewed here. These comments are designed to illustrate the actual comments of a real interview, and so no attempt is made to present them in grammatically correct form or as complete sentences. As such, they are the interviewer's written impressions from the interview with Mr. Block.

Rapport/introduction. Makes a positive first impression. He is well dressed, dark suit, polished shoes, recently cut hair. Looks physically fit and may work out on some regular basis; slight military bearing. Solid handshake, maintains eye contact, and walks with a semi-determined but respectful manner.

Early childhood. Says grew up in "middle-class environment." Father was accountant for manufacturing firm, mother a "housewife." Two younger brothers, all college graduates, each doing well. Comfortable, but far from rich.

Work experiences. Paper route early on—had to earn own "spending money." Worked some summers (along with military obligation) for college spending money. Considered military career but wanted faster career advancement and did not attend naval academy so would always be considered "second best." Claims rapid promotion based on sales ability and record, but no openings for him in management so change.

Activities. College fraternity, pledge trainer, and president. Says was "strong" leader and popular. Now plays basketball and baseball in leagues. Describes self as average ability but he "works at it."

Self-description. Disciplined, politely aggressive, and eager to lead others to achieve goals.

Planning and organizing. 120 Questionnaire is very thorough. Expresses self in complete sentences and generally correct syntax, etc. Also general responses seem to indicate some overachiever and aggressive—discipline, hard work, control, and leading by example.

Judgment and decisiveness. Indicates that his judgment is maturing, especially in leading "nonmilitary" types. Accustomed to command without questions being asked. Definitely decisive. Claims he "lives" with any decision he makes and almost never looks back.

Delegation. Says he will do it, but I tend to doubt it. He likes to keep the final approval for himself. He tends to be more interested in building something that reflects well on his working through others rather than with others. Probably high aggressive and some compulsive but generally average minus active.

Adaptability. Says he "can" live with change. But he prefers to "plan his work and then work his plan."

Drive. Appears highly driven and interested in attaining a position beyond his level of social maturity. He appears to be in a race with himself to reach some level of accomplishment by time X. But he would not comment on this. Could be high entrepreneur, but I don't think he is necessarily money-driven; more driven to see if he can accomplish his goals.

Persuasive. Individually yes. He is in command of himself, and by sheer sense of determination and devotion to duty he will accomplish his goals. This can inspire others (clients) to have confidence in him. So yes, he is persuasive, but not necessarily clever, insightful, or interpersonally engaging. High aggressive, low active, average entrepreneur.

Summary. Mr. Block is highly self-disciplined, controlled, and driven to achieve his goals. This picture is apparent from first meeting him—his neat, trim, military appearance—and was confirmed during the meeting. He plays sports in a league to maintain his physical condition and a sense of mental discipline. He has worked hard from a fairly early age and earned his own spending money in high school and college. The ROTC scholarship was a way to pay for college.

His academic grades reflect his desire to do well against some standard of measurement. He says "he could have done better" but wanted some balance in his life—fraternity, social life, and so on. He sets goals and then strives to achieve them almost for the sake of meeting his own expectations. He finished every academic program he started. He is proud of his ability in sales and sees it as a testament to his perseverance and work-related diligence. He does not take the first "no" and yet indicates that he is politely persuasive.

So he is conscious of being overly aggressive and consciously disciplines himself to persuade through his own self-perceived self-confidence rather than by being outwardly aggressive and possibly intimidating. This could be a fine line, but he appears to possess more overachiever than aggressive in his temperament; however, he may come across as being too pushy, especially in the fairly soft-sell environment of the food industry. Conclusion: high overachiever rating.

He is competitive in the athletic sense of the word, but not so much for money as for the pure sense of achievement. He seldom mentions money as a factor, and his attitude seemed more concerned with discipline and social power (overachiever-aggressive) than with individual recognition for his efforts. He likes money as a way of keeping score but appears to think that if he builds a successful sales unit, the money will come as a result of that effort. He played team sports and readily admitted that he was a contributor rather than a leader in these activities.

He plays sports to stay in shape and to compete within the group. He is not seeking separate recognition or the individual spotlight for these efforts. He is competitive but thoroughly honest and completely aboveboard. He is not Machiavellian, clever, or necessarily shrewd. He is generally aware of these traits in others but does not appear to use them as part of his behavior pattern or presentation style. He is more a "straight-ahead" person. Conclusion: an average rating on the entrepreneur trait.

He is highly energetic but only moderately (emotionally) enthusiastic; that is, he is a team player, but he may ultimately insist on being a team leader. He insists, however, on being thought of as a regular team sort of guy. I'm not sure I believe it, not that he is deliberately lying about his desire to be a team player, but I think his ambition to lead the group is much stronger than his interest in being with the group. His attitude does not show much natural warmth. His present employer has not given him a management role yet.

His references to management in the military and college are weak. He is very strong-willed and may be effective managing a production line where he can bark orders, but he may need some people-handling experiences before being given responsibility for motivating and leading a sales force. He can lead the way and shows plenty of energy—all his activities in college and even currently—but can he charismatically lead? Conclusion: average minus score on the active.

There is very little evidence to suggest that he is high on the passive and sensitized traits. He is very action-oriented, determined, and self-directed. He is not given to daydreaming, polite consideration of "what-if" issues, or consideration for people without individual ambition. He is not necessarily insensitive or uncompassionate; however, he sees "direct" and, if necessary, "forceful" action as the best way to achieve his goals. Conclusion: low ratings for the passive and sensitized traits.

He wants to be in charge and may be a credible leader of a carefully defined task; however, he lacks natural warmth, social enthusiasm, and obvious team spirit/camaraderie. He is determined, and, like a rocket heading for a target, he can have difficulty changing his mind. He prefers to plan his work and work his plan. He can be one-dimensional and possibly overly concerned with achieving his objectives—almost without consideration that other parts of the organization can also reach theirs. He is surprisingly detail-minded, organized, and systematic. This trait is obvious from the 120 Questionnaire responses, and his presentation style is matter-of-fact, highly focused, and direct. He can be somewhat overpowering in his delivery. Conclusion: high scores on the aggressive and at least average plus for the compulsive.

He may be a great sales manager for young people who will accept his guidance (instructions), but the more mature sales reps may (and probably

Chart 7.3
Person Analysis Chart—John Block

	Low		Medium		High	
	– – – – – – – –		5		+ + + + + + +	
Overachiever	/////////////////////					
Entrepreneur	/////////////					
Active	/////					
Passive	//					
Sensitized	/					
Aggressive	/////////////////////////////////////					
Compulsive	///////////////////////////					

will) resent his youth, aggressiveness, and potentially overbearing manner. He could be successful with us if given a small team of fairly new sales reps, and he could (with proper guidance) mature into a more rounded and socially responsive sales manager in two or three years, but placing him in this position now is a risk. I will check impressions with others, but, currently, I am guardedly optimistic about his chances with us in the position. As an interviewer of Mr. Block, my final impressions of his seven behavior traits are graphed in Chart 7.3.

120 Questionnaire—
Application Blank

This appendix contains a copy of a blank 120 Questionnaire, which is one of the building blocks for understanding the entire system of interviewing described in this book. This questionnaire is designed to serve as an application form and should be completed by the candidate before he is seen for an in-depth interview. It is important for the candidate to complete the entire questionnaire, even though it may repeat information already contained on the resume.

At first glance it might appear that there is little to learn from a blank questionnaire, but this perception would be wrong. The questionnaire is included here to provide the interviewer an appreciation for how the candidate feels when he first sees it. Moreover, the interest, respect, and value the interviewer places on the blank questionnaire will influence the manner in which the candidate completes it. For example, if the interviewer suggests that it is just "some form" that the personnel department requires as part of the hiring process, then the candidate may respond in kind. In this case, he may be less inclined to provide you the meaningful information that the questionnaire is designed to elicit. On the other hand, consider that the interviewer tells the candidate "I like what I see in you so far, but I would like you to complete this form to provide me with some additional info. Would you mind taking the time to complete it?" or "As part of our sales selection process every candidate is required to complete this form. It can require one–two hours, but if you are serious about a position with us, we ask you to complete it. You can either take it home and mail it back to us or fill it out in the next office." Both of these messages convey a much higher level of interest in the candidate, and he will probably provide more meaningful results.

The question numbers place the individual's questions in the context of the entire questionnaire.

DIRECTIONS for COMPLETING the QUESTIONNAIRE

The questionnaire is designed to enable you to tell us about yourself, your education, work history, attitudes and perceptions. It is not a test. Please answer all questions accurately and completely. Nothing on this form is intended for discriminatory purposes. Supply no information that would identify age, race, color, creed, ancestry, national origin, religion, sex, marital status or mental or physical disability.

Last Name _____ M.I. _____ First _____

Home Address _____

City_____ State_____ Zip Code_____ Phone # (___) _____

Social Security Number _____ Date _____

Company Sponsoring This Exercise _____

Person _____ Title _____

Company Address _____

City_____ State _____ Zip Code_____ Phone # (___)_____

Describe your development. What factors (family, education, work, etc.) influenced you to be the person that you are today?_____
_____
_____
_____
_____
_____
_____
_____
_____
_____

Copyright 1987, James B. Weitzul, Ph.D.

Level	Name and Location	Major and Minor Courses (If any)	Date From/To	Diploma or Degree	Average Grade
High School					
College					
Night School					
Other					
Other					

Did you interrupt or fail to finish any level of your education? If so, please explain: _____

_____

_____

_____

What were your favorite courses in school?_____

_____

Why did they appeal to you?_____

_____

_____

_____

What courses gave you the most trouble?_____

_____

Why do you think you had problems with them?_____

_____

_____

_____

What other courses or supplementary instruction would you like to pursue?_____

_____

_____

Which of your teachers had the most effect on you? Tell us why you remember him or her so well.

_____

_____

_____

Which extracurricular activities were you involved in, while in school or college? List clubs, organizations, sports, academic events, music, offices, etc. _____

_____

_____

_____

_____

What honors, prizes, distinctions, etc. have you earned? _____

_____

_____

How did you pay for your education (family, scholarship or grant, loan, G.I. Bill, job earnings, etc.)? Please give particulars. _____

_____

_____

_____

Which of your jobs or posts did you enjoy the most? Why? _____

_____

_____

_____

_____

_____

Name of Employer	Where Employed	Nature of Business	Describe Position and Duties	Immediate Superior

Which of your jobs or posts did you enjoy least? Why? _____
_____
_____

Select any company or firm for which you have worked and relate its feeling and position towards people. _____
_____
_____
_____

What part-time, temporary or off-season jobs, not included below, did you have as a youth?_____
_____
_____

What kind of work would you enjoy doing 5 years from now? How much would you want to earn then? _____
_____
_____
_____
_____
_____

Dates Of Employment		Monthly Income			Please explain reason for leaving or desiring to leave
From	To	Start	Present or Last	Salary or Commission	

Describe your favorite boss or supervisor for us, (temperament, techniques, outlook, etc.)._____

_____

_____

_____

_____

_____

_____

_____

Tell us about the boss or supervisor that you found the hardest to work for, (temperament, techniques, outlook, etc.)._____

_____

_____

_____

_____

_____

For which jobs or posts would you be most capable? Please specify abilities or skills. _____

_____

_____

_____

_____

_____

Please describe a major work accomplishment (what, when, how)?_____

_____

_____

_____

_____

_____

_____

What do you read on a regular basis? _____

_____

_____

How do you spend your spare time? (sports or exercise, pastimes, clubs or groups, etc.) On the average, how much time do you allow for each in a normal week? _____

_____

_____

What work related groups are you a member of? Please specify any offices that you may hold or have held. _____

_____

_____

Please give us an example of a work related conflict situation. What happened, who involved, how resolved? _____

_____

_____

_____

_____

_____

_____

As a youngster, did anyone inspire you to achieve your goals? Who, what did they do? _____

_____

_____

_____

_____

_____

_____

_____

_____

How would you describe yourself today (how do you look at life, what do you like best about your-self and where are you not as strong, etc.)?_____

_____

_____

_____

_____

_____

_____

What would you like to accomplish in the future (goals, ambitions, projects, etc.)? _____

_____

_____

_____

_____

_____

Rank the following goals in the order of importance for you. Give the highest a "1" and so on.

( )   *affection--sharing feelings with others and being appreciated by them*

( )   *duty--meeting obligations to the best of your ability*

( )   *expertise--being effective at what you do*

( )   *independence--having freedom to think and act according to your own wishes*

( )   *leadership--taking responsibility for a group project and making sure it is accomplished*

( )   *pleasure--finding contentment in life*

( )   *entrepreneureal drive--owning or supervising a business as if it were your own*

( )   *prestige--gaining a reputation as being one of the "best" in your area*

( )   *security--having a stable work position*

( )   *self-realization--developing yourself to the fullest*

( )   *service--helping satisfy others*

( )   *money--earning enough income to satisfy your needs and enjoy some "extras" occaisionally*

Please complete the following phrases to make sentences.

When working with others

I feel jealous when

Those under me

I work best when

What people don't like about me

When I'm not doing something well

I want to

Supervisors ought to

My best trait is

When things don't go well

When I'm mad

People like me best for

When things don't work out as I hoped

I find it difficult to

What most makes me feel good is

Power over people

Money is

When depressed I

Independence is

Supervisors usually

Working on fine points

Showing feelings

Bright people often

To be on good terms with people in a group

When by myself

Sometimes I

I'm not sure about my

My creative skills

On a team my role is

Speaking in front of a group

When criticized for my work, I

When I don't agree with most people

If my superior could

When asked to do what I'd rather not

When I must wait, I

I close up when

Being secure means

I get excited when

I feel that money

After saying what I really feel, I

I was most disappointed with my work when

When I have to get work finished by

People I like least

I most like my

I like having a lot of time for

Self discipline is something that

220 Questionnaire— Interview Questions

This appendix introduces the 220 Questionnaire (interviewer questions) in the form of a blank questionnaire. It should be read along with chapter 6; the two chapters are complementary.

The 220 Questionnaire is a separate booklet containing a number of questions that the interviewer can ask the candidate during the interview. The questions have been carefully researched and developed over a long period of time. They are designed to elicit specific information from a candidate that the interviewer can then use to determine the candidate's behavior style and interpersonal skills. It may require some time to become comfortable with the questions, but using them will lead to an improved understanding of the candidate and better interviewing.

It is assumed that the candidate has completed the 120 Questionnaire and the interviewer has reviewed it. This assumption is important because the value of using the 220 Questionnaire builds on the knowledge gained by reviewing the candidate's responses to the 120 Questionnaire.

The contents of the 220 Questionnaire are arranged around a number of specific topics that are designed to help the interviewer improve his analysis of the candidate's level of interpersonal skill. By reviewing the candidate's responses to questions about each of these topics, the interviewer can gain a better appreciation of the candidate's general abilities and gain a more complete understanding of him as a person. This improved understanding comes about because the interviewer can ask these questions of a candidate and compare the candidate's responses with the responses from individuals representing the different behavior traits introduced in chapter 2.

The chapter begins with a brief introduction about the use of questions during an interview and then discloses that the 220 Questionnaire is composed of approximately 220 questions. It has 22 sections of approximately

10 questions each. The questionnaire is further divided into four parts as follows:

- Part 1: Introduction (sections 10–20)
- Part 2: Background (sections 30–70)
- Part 3: Temperament (sections 80–200)
- Part 4: Conclusion (sections 210–220)

INTRODUCTION

The purpose of these questions is to assist you more effectively understand a given candidate's general behavior style and in particular to rate his interpersonal skills. During the interview there is no need to ask the questions exactly as described here nor to ask every question listed. It is recommended, however, that the interviewer review all of the questions and then begin to select and modify them for each interview.

Part 1 of the 220 Questionnaire contains sections 10–20. It briefly lists some questions to introduce the process, establish rapport, and establish a sense of trust and openness during the interview. It then shifts to the purpose of your meeting—the interview.

Part 2 of the 220 Questionnaire lists a series of questions that enable the interviewer to review the information the candidate has provided on the 120 Questionnaire. The topics in this section include a review of the candidate's biographical background. These questions cover the topics that the candidate has supplied written answers for in the 120 Questionnaire. We ask about these areas again for two purposes: first, to check the accuracy of the candidate's written responses and second, to clarify and further explore the whys and wherefores of the candidate's written responses.

That is, we are interested in discovering the candidate's attitude about completing his education and the nuances of his life experiences at school and work, not just the dates of his attendance and some of his stated activities. For example, the candidate may indicate on the 120 Questionnaire that he left job A on date 1 for a "better opportunity," but under the inherent semistress conditions of an interview, he may indicate that he actually left job A on date 2 and that he was terminated for lack of sales production.

Part 3 of the 220 Questionnaire further explores the candidate's temperament. The questions in this section can be used to explore further the whys and wherefores of the candidate's behavior. These questions are further designed to allow us to understand the candidate's behavior style and level of interpersonal skill development. That is, we ask about planning and organizing because we can compare the candidate's responses to these questions to the responses of other candidates whose behavior styles (and interpersonal skill levels) are known. In this way, we then partly determine the candidate's interpersonal skill level. In particular, this topic provides a measure of the candidate's overachiever and compulsive traits. In a similar vein, the candidate's responses to the risk-taking questions can be used to define further his degree of the entrepreneurial trait. These and other interpretations of responses to the 220 Questionnaire are discussed in chapter 6.

Look at the topics in Part 3 that you feel are appropriate for the position being considered. Many of these questions can be used in combination with questions listed in Part 2. That is, they are intended to be used as follow-up questions to specific Part 2 questions, or they can be asked separately after you have reviewed the candidate's background. For example, a number of questions dealing with these temperament topics are designed to be asked while reviewing the candidate's school years and/or work history. These are obvious follow-up questions.

If these questions are asked after the general review of the candidate's background, then you probably want to say something like: "I'd like to get some specific information about your experience in certain areas. Please tell me about your experiences in planning and organizing activities." Then continue asking the candidate the questions that will reveal the information that you need to know.

The material is presented here in this fashion as a means of organizing it for the reader. Once the interviewer is familiar with the material, the questions should be combined and integrated into an overall and comprehensive interview schedule; however, this combination can be started only after a complete understanding of, and appreciation for, each section is gained.

Part 4 of the 220 Questionnaire deals with the appropriate way to conclude the interview. This important topic is sometimes overlooked by the interviewer but can be very important to the candidate, so it is wise to conclude the interview carefully.

The section numbers and the question topics are as follows:

	Section Number	Question Topic
Part 1	Introduction	
	10	Establish rapport
	20	Introduction
Part 2	Background	
	30	Early childhood
	40	Education
	50	Work experience
	60	Activities
	70	Self-description
Part 3	Temperament	
	80	Planning and organizing

	90	Problem analysis
	100	Judgment and decisiveness
	110	Risk taking
	120	Delegation
	130	Follow-up and control
	140	Drive
	150	Self-esteem
	160	Self-development
	170	Stress tolerance
	180	Adaptability
	190	Persuasiveness
	200	Communication
Part 4	Conclusion	
	210	Information on company
	220	Conclusion

PART 1: INTRODUCTION

Establish Rapport

The introductory questions are designed to help the candidate to relax and feel comfortable in your presence. You may want to begin by asking the candidate about the trip to your office, possible use of the washroom, or a cup of coffee, tea, or soda.

Introduction

Generally we recommend a transition comment here like, "Well, I'm pleased that we have X in common, but we had better get down to the business at hand. Let's start the interview process, OK?"

PART 2: BACKGROUND

Early Childhood

Did your early childhood affect your later development? How?

Do you have any brothers and/or sisters? Where do you place in the order?

As best as you can recall, what was your early childhood like?

Education

Let's change focus to your school years. Please describe your high school years.

What were your activities and interests?

Did you, for example, play any sports or participate in the band or any social clubs?

How did you perform academically?

Do you resent not going to college? Or, if appropriate, do you resent not completing college?

How has this experience influenced you?

How did you select X college?

Did you live away from home?

Work Experience

Let's look at your work experience since finishing school. Please start with your first full-time job and describe each position to me—whom you worked for, the dates, what you did, how you did it, why you left each company, and so on.

What things did you like best? Why?

What activities did you like least? Why?

What are some of your major work accomplishments?

Please describe a difficult problem that you faced. What was the situation? What was the outcome? What did you learn from it?

How did you get promoted?

What sorts of challenges did the job entail?

How was your performance rated?

Please describe your best/worst supervisor.

What frustrations did you feel on the job? What did you do to relieve them?

What kind of work environment do you work best in?

What are you looking for in a job/career?

Activities

Your work obviously keeps you pretty busy, but do you have any spare-time activities, hobbies, and interests?

Community involvement/volunteer activities? Any leadership role?

What did you learn from activities?

Given the outside commitment that you have, what about relocation, travel, weekend work, nights, and so on? Any problems?

Self-Description

How would you summarize everything you have told me so far? That is, can you give me a comprehensive description of yourself?

How would others (your bosses, peers, subordinates) describe you? Please use three words for each group.

What are the accomplishments that you are most proud of?

Have you had any failures? or significant setbacks?

What specific talents can you bring to the job, company?

What areas do you need to improve in?

Do you need/want any additional training in a given area?

What sorts of programs or experiences do you want to be exposed to?

Have you been consistently told to improve in any one area? What is it? What are your plans for change?

PART 3: TEMPERAMENT

Questions to Determine Planning and Organization Skills

How did you develop an interest in_____? (course of study)

If the candidate paid for a major portion of his own education, ask him how he managed his work/study and maintained a social life.

If his career seems to be taking a different tack from his education, ask him how he happened to get into_____.

If there are a number of extracurricular activities listed, ask him how he managed his time. If not listed, ask him if he had any outside interests.

How do you schedule your time at work? Is it necessary to set priorities in your job? How do you do that?

Do you have a set procedure for keeping track of things requiring your attention?

How do you decide what to give your attention to first on a day-to-day or weekly basis?

Did you have objectives for your department last year? What did you have to do to ensure they were met?

What do you think of management by objectives?

Describe how you determine what constitutes top priority in your job.

How would you improve the planning system in your department?

Interview Questions for Problem Analysis Skills

There are many decisions that a person has to make (or that are made for him) to get to the current point in his life. Any or all of these are subject to exploration. Human beings are distinguished from other animals by their ability to make rational choices beyond the level of mere survival. To determine the level of one's problem analysis skills, look at the means by which an individual has gone about exercising his choices.

The key questions to ask are "why," "what," and "how." Why did you do that? On what basis did you decide? To what do you attribute that? How do you know that is true?

What did you enjoy about your paper route? Why?

What did you like about school? Dislike? Why?

Why did you join the Boy Scouts?

To what do you attribute your success in school?

Why did you leave home at age 18?

How did you decide to play football?

What is important to you in life? What happened to cause you to decide that?

How did you decide to join the military?

What goals have you set? Why?

How did you select your college? Major?

What would you change about your current position if you had the authority? Why?

What appeals to you about the company? The X industry?

What distinguishes the company from other companies in this industry?

What do you plan to do to accomplish your goals? What do you anticipate will be the difference between your present job and the one for which you are applying? Describe the toughest problem you've had to solve. How did you go about solving it?

Questions to Determine Judgment and Decisiveness

More decisive people, as well as more intelligent people, tend to respond to questions more quickly. When open-ended questions are posed, they will decide how they are going to respond rather than constantly ask for clarification. They tend to be able to shift subjects more quickly in response to questions. They are as definite in their response to opinion questions as they are to factual questions. In general, they demonstrate more social self-confidence and are more sure of themselves. Measuring a person on this category is not so much a function of what the candidate says, but how he says it.

Questions to Determine Risk Taking

To be successful as a manager, what percentage of your decisions must be correct?

Describe a recent decision having more than the usual element of risk.

Describe a decision you have had to make when you did not have all the pertinent data.

What do you do when you receive a new procedure or instruction with which you disagree?

Tell me about the most risky decision you have ever made. How long did it take you to gather the information and to make the decision?

Questions to Determine Delegation Skills

How many people reported to you?

To whom did you, or do you, delegate?

How do you decide to whom you delegate?

What happens when things you have delegated do not get done?

What kinds of things do you delegate?

What don't you delegate?

What is the difference between delegating authority and delegating responsibility?

What kinds of decisions do you delegate to your subordinates?

How much time do you work?

Questions to Determine Follow-up and Control Skills

If you had five salespersons reporting to you who had territories at least 100 miles away, how would you know what they were doing?

When you delegate work, how do you know it gets done properly?

What methods do you usually use to keep informed about what is going on in your area of responsibility?

How do you monitor the quality of the work done by your subordinates?

What type of report do you find most helpful in monitoring the progress of your area of responsibility? How do you use the report?

What kinds of meetings do you have and what is covered?

How does your superior know how well you are doing?

What did you like about the best boss you have had?

Questions to Determine Drive

When interviewing an individual whose academic performance was average or mediocre, ask the following questions:

If you were in school now, what, if anything, would you do differently?

Is your level of achievement in school indicative of your current level of performance on the job?

If no: When did achieving become important to you? To what do you attribute your change in attitude?

What have you done in your work that was above or beyond expectation in your job description?

What is success to you?

To what do you attribute your success in_____?

What are your aspirations? (How well-defined and realistic?)

Do you consider yourself to be a self-starter? (The answer is always yes.) Describe projects you've started that were not assigned or necessarily expected of you.

How do you know when you've done a good job?

What has been your most satisfying experience on the job?

What has been your most dissatisfying experience on the job?

Note one of the areas of his job he dislikes and ask: How do you handle _____ ?

In what ways have you developed personally in the last year or two?

What have you done to increase the responsibilities of your present position?

What do you think is the most important responsibility of your current position?

In what ways did you extend yourself to meet the requirements of your most challenging position?

How did you handle your least favorite position?

Questions to Determine Self-Esteem

Many observations can be made about a person's level of self-esteem without asking particular questions. There are a few questions that can be used to reveal information in this area:

What do you consider to be your personal strengths and areas requiring development?

To what do you attribute your ability to get along with others?

Tell me about the last time you made a major mistake on the job.

What kinds of people or particular traits about others annoy you?

In what ways do you feel you could improve your performance on the job?

How would you describe your character?

How do you see your character in 5 or 10 years?

Have you recognized flaws in yourself, or were they pointed out to you by others?

How do you recognize flaws in yourself?

In what way have you ever disappointed yourself?

Do you feel that your coworkers are confident of your ability?

To whom or what do you attribute that confidence or lack thereof?

From what type of person do you find it easiest to learn?

From what type of person do you find it easiest to take criticism?

What is the most recent skill you have learned?

What skill would you like to acquire?

What is the latest challenge you have met?

At what level of success would you be satisfied?

Thirty years from now how do you see yourself spending your spare time?

Questions to Determine Self-Development Orientation

Have you identified any areas, in the last year or two, that you felt you could improve? If so, what have you done to improve?

How do you identify those areas in which you feel you need to improve?

Who, if anyone, has had the most influence on your personal development? In what ways?

What do you typically do when you discover you have made a mistake?

How do you feel when mistakes are pointed out to you?

How do you feel you could have improved your performance on your last job? In school?

What are your aspirations? What would you like to be doing five years from now? What are you doing to prepare for the future?

Are you satisfied with yourself the way you are now, or do you feel you could be more successful? In what ways do you feel you could be more successful?

In what areas do you feel you need to improve in order to become a manager?

What is your best friend most likely to criticize about you? How do you feel about this criticism? What do you plan to do about it?

Describe the best boss or teacher you have ever had. Why was he the best? What, if any, characteristics do you feel he had that you lack?

To what do you attribute your greatest success and/or failure?

Would you say that you have been lucky in your professional life? How?

At what time in your career would you say luck played an important role?

How do you define success?

What is your superior's attitude toward you and your coworkers?

What type of personality do you feel is ideal for a manager?

Questions to Determine Stress Tolerance

Although the interview itself provides considerable opportunity to evaluate stress, the following questions can be used if needed.

Under what conditions do you do your best work?

Do you feel pressure in your job? How do you handle it?

What is your reaction when others lose their tempers or become irritated with you?

What, if anything, causes you to lose your temper?

How does your spouse or family feel about your working long hours?

Describe the most difficult person you have ever had to deal with. How did you handle him?

What kinds of people are you most likely to become impatient with? How do you deal with them?

What kinds of problems annoy you the most?

What existing conditions within your current job are most frustrating to you? How do you handle them?

How do you feel when a superior becomes angry with you?

How do you handle it?

How do you handle it when a client becomes angry with you?

What type of problems annoy you the most?

Do you feel that you effectively deal with the anger?

What situations make you nervous?

Would you describe your position as a stressful one?

What situations make you impatient?

What is the most frustrating aspect of your job?

How do you handle your frustration?

Questions to Determine Adaptability

If the interviewee has had a leadership position in a college or civic organization, ask him how he was able to get people to work and how that might differ from getting people to work for him when he had authority.

Describe two different management styles, either yours and a boss's, or two bosses you have had.

What are the key obstacles you have had to accomplishing your objectives in your job? How have you dealt with them?

Describe an incident where you disagreed with your boss. How was it settled?

How effective has your organization been in adapting its policies to a changing environment?

Give me an example of when a suggestion from another person influenced your decision. And when it did not.

Have you changed geographical locations often? How do you feel about moving? What problems might it cause for you or your family?

Could you become comfortable in a foreign country if you were asked to relocate?

How do you handle a difficult client?

Can you speak comfortably to a large group?

If a client is not responding to your arguments, do you change your approach?

How do you decide what approach you will take with a client?

How well do you and your department adapt to new supervisors or job responsibilities?

Describe what you consider to be an effective management style and an ineffective management style.

How long does it take for you to become comfortable in a new place?

Can others influence your decisions?

Are you often open to suggestion when faced with a dilemma?

Questions to Determine Persuasiveness

The interviewer should ordinarily be able to assess persuasive skills without asking particular questions. On the 120 Questionnaire, look for situations that would ordinarily require the individual to be persuasive to accomplish his objectives. Look for leadership positions of any kind, management or sales experience; positions where he has authority versus voluntary efforts. During the interview, attend to characteristics noted above. Following are a few specific questions if needed.

What is the best idea you have presented to a superior or another person? Why did he/she buy it?

Describe the best idea you tried to sell that was not accepted. Why wasn't it? What did you do?

If you were in a staff position, what would be the best way to get line or operating people to accept your ideas?

Have you ever had to give a speech or report before a group? What were you trying to accomplish? How did it go?

Are you good at getting other people to do what you want them to do? (Must follow up): How do you do it?

If subject has had supervisory experience:

How do you motivate your subordinates to perform more effectively?

How do you go about criticizing a subordinate or another person?

Are you willing to take an unpopular stand? (Must follow up): Why or on what basis? Have you ever done it? What was the result?

In what ways, if any, do you feel you could improve your ability to sell yourself or your ideas?

Describe the last time you persuaded an employee to do something.

If your presentation is not being well received, do you change your approach?

What aspect of your position do you feel commands the most respect from your employees?

Communication

There are no specific questions to ask for this section; however, communication is definitely a skill that can be rated during the interview. This rating is based on an overall impression of the candidate's communication skill. This rating is discussed in more detail in chapter 8.

PART 4: CONCLUSION

Information on the Company

This portion of the interview is typically important to the candidate. Therefore, you want to be both careful and explicit in what you say. You want to convey a certain sense of professional warmth and concern, but you also need to be factual and specific in your comments. Some of the topics you may wish to cover include information about the company and any general career opportunities, the possibility for additional training, the general benefits package, the job location, and any requirements for travel or overtime. Finally, you may wish to state the salary range.

Conclusion

This section should be for any unfinished business. A good way to start this section is to say something like: "Well, I think we have about covered everything. Do you have any questions about us, the job, or anything else that I can answer?" Then ask about the candidate's level of interest in the company and review the next step in the interviewing process, for example, "We will be getting back to you by the end of the week." Finally, close with an appropriate comment like, "I would like to thank you for coming in today and giving me this chance to visit. We'll be in touch."

Appendix C

320 Questionnaire— Temperament Measure

The completed answer sheet to this questionnaire may be mailed to:

James B. Weitzul, Ph.D.
Banks & Weitzul, Inc.
P.O. Box 2351
Princeton, NJ 08540.

However, please contact Dr. Weitzul *before* doing so.

DIRECTIONS FOR COMPLETING THE QUESTIONNAIRE

This questionnaire is designed to enable you to relate how you feel about some descriptive statements. Read each question carefully and answer it "yes" by placing an X in the box marked yes or answer it "no" by placing an X in the box marked no. There are no "right or wrong" answers to these questions, but, generally, the first answer that comes to you is the better answer.

PLEASE DO NOT WRITE IN THIS BOOKLET

COPYRIGHT 1987 James B. Weitzul, Ph.D.

1. Do you map out a strategy for problems and then carry out the strategy step by step?
2. Do you find you must be by yourself when you're worried or disturbed?
3. Do you avoid discussing issues that are close to your heart?
4. Have there been certain periods in your life when the meaning of existence was unmistakably plain to you?
5. Did you ever receive low marks for deportment when you were in school?

6. If a person is constantly pestering you, do you restrain yourself for as long as you can and then explode?

7. If you desire to reach the top, do you feel you must be on good terms with those who already have power or status?

8. Do you have more worries than the majority of people?

9. Do you discover that your superiors many times lack your knowledge of your job?

10. Has there ever been a stage in your life when for days, weeks or months you couldn't muster the drive to take care of any business?

11. Have you ever been bothered by difficulties to the extent that you saw no real way of escaping them?

12. Are there certain days when you feel more ready to get involved than other days?

13. Do you frequently feel obligated to defend what you hold true?

14. Do some people think of you as hot-tempered?

15. Will you at times doubt or suspect a physician if he claims you're in good health and you don't agree?

16. Are you frequently preoccupied or apprehensive about any matter?

17. Do you ever experience tension or stress in the head or neck regions?

18. Do you relate to people so well that your favorite activity is to socialize?

19. Do others regard you as economical and thrifty?

20. Are you blunt and straight to the point with those who, in your opinion, should change their ways?

21. When people seem especially agreeable or amicable, is it the best policy to be on your guard?

22. Do you have an associate or companion who exploits you without your minding?

23. Are you likely to avoid doing something for yourself because no one agrees with you?

24. Have you ever thought that you were unsuccessful at everything you tried, almost useless?

25. Will you refrain from acting on your convictions because of what other people might say?

26. Do you suffer from migraine headaches that are concentrated on one side of your head?

27. Do you seldom voice a conviction or deeply held belief?

28. Are you ever so embarrassed that you blush?

29. Do you have sudden fits of inspiration that spur you on to finish important projects?

30. Do a sizable number of people exaggerate their problems in order to elicit pity and help?

31. Do you feel vindicated if your ideas turn out to be correct, even when they aren't carried out?

32. Have you ever lost consciousness from any cause?

33. Are your actions determined by what is customary and normal?

34. In a business transaction, are you shrewd and quick-witted most of the time?

35. Do you return to your house to make sure of certain things like turning off all the heaters or stoves?

36. Have others ever misconstrued your efforts when you tried to show them how to avoid mistakes?

37. Are you so eager and involved at times that you create problems for yourself?

38. Do you have a personal world of your own in your imagination?

39. Is your life free of emotional problems?

40. Do you have to combat your own modesty or bashfulness at times?

41. Are you very annoyed when you find out that others are talking about you?

42. Do you force yourself to keep quiet about vital concerns, even though your friends express their views?

43. Do failures or setbacks affect you so much that you are unable to put them aside?

44. Are there particular people who have an uncanny way of irritating you?

45. Do you ignore the bad points about your friends because of your friendship?

46. Has an idea ever suddenly occurred to you that allowed you to prepare a sweeping design for a major project?

47. Have you ever taken a dangerous risk merely for the thrill of it?

48. Do you like to see someone who has been duped or victimized get the upper hand over a criminal or cheat?

49. Do you become apprehensive if you're in a boat or ship?

50. Do you feel apprehensive if you are alone in a large expanse?

51. Do you enjoy putting things over on people by exaggerating or stretching the truth?

52. At a social gathering do you make a special effort to get people relaxed and comfortable?

53. Do you maintain silence unless you are requested to speak, even though a conference or talk is not working out?

54. Have you ever accepted work where concentration on the small points was the only important aspect of the job?

55. Does it disturb you to participate in games or sports for which you are not skilled?

56. Are there any particular animals that unnerve you?

57. Do you keep your temper even when others annoy or bait you?

58. If you and several friends ran into trouble, would you agree that all of you should plan out a common version of the incident?

59. Do you enjoy dealing with one matter at a time, rather than many things happening around you at one time?

60. Do you frequently have so much work on your hands that you almost can't decide where to begin?

61. Do you feel that "what works for the majority will work for all" is a good code of personal behavior?

62. As a rule of thumb, is it immoral to swindle a person if he or she is out to swindle you?

63. If you get into difficulty, do you omit certain facts to protect yourself?

64. Have you ever come up with a sudden idea that permitted you to make important plans with great confidence?

65. Have you ever retaliated against someone not so much to gain revenge, but because it was the right thing to do?

66. Have you ever worked for a long while with someone you disliked or pitied without telling the person what you personally thought?

67. Do you ever feel dejected to the point that you barely feel like trying anymore?

68. If you and your friends all shared in the responsibility for something, would you accept all the blame for yourself rather than implicate them?

69. Would most persons pass up their opportunity if they had to use foul play to seize it?

70. Have you ever purchased more on time payments than you could afford?

71. When you hear about a friend's success, do you compare his achievement to your own and view yourself as inferior?

72. Do the majority of individuals choose their friends while thinking about the practical value of the relationship?

73. If you and an equally qualified person were competing for the same position, would you feel right about getting on better terms with your superior to gain the promotion?

74. Are others more obedient and dutiful if you bear down on them from time to time?

75. Are you quick to take up a good idea and completely believe in its worth?

76. Has any person ever hoodwinked you so completely that you had to acknowledge the job was well done?

77. When you are trying to solve a major problem, are you bothered when another person requires you to decide another issue?

78. Do setbacks have a way of making you feel low-spirited?

79. When you encounter people you don't know, is it difficult for you to start a conversation?

80. Did you ever feel that persons who were not acquaintances of yours were finding fault with you?

81. Do you easily become red in the face if you are complimented or if you're confused?

82. Is persuading people of the truth a laborious task?

83. Have you ever feigned illness or an accident to obtain your goals with friends or fellow employees?

84. Do you ever find yourself thinking that you are inferior to your friends?

85. Do you at times feel out-of-sorts or peevish without any specific cause?

86. Are you timid to the extent that at times you wait to speak up when you know your position is the correct one?

87. Do others frequently disappoint you?

88. Do you prefer following your own methods even if other procedures are more customary?

89. When an especially domineering person gives you an order, do you feel like totally contradicting his request, even though he's correct?

90. Are you understanding of people who apparently lack the power to forget their problems and move ahead?

91. Does waiting make you fidgety and impatient?

92. As a child, did you enjoy whatever was daring and thrilling?

93. Do you have secrets or private matters you could never discuss with anyone else?

94. Have you had the experience several times that another person has accepted the recognition for concepts that originated with you?

95. When you become wrapped up in something, do you have difficulty letting the project rest so you can see to other concerns?

96. Do others become irritated with you because of your perseverance or tenacity?

97. When a person offends or bothers you, do you intentionally disregard what he does rather than strike back at him?

98. Have you failed to capitalize on your opportunities as a result of waiting too long?

99. Do you feel tense and uneasy if you're up before a considerable number of people?

100. Do you ignore or repress negative ideas and perceptions?

101. When a person is friendly or pleasant to you, do you try to determine his or her motives?

102. Do you feel angry if a person is convicted and then released on the basis of a legal technicality?

103. Were you very energetic and lively as a child?

104. Do you feel that a large number of people are immoral?

105. Do you attempt to get others to accept your religious beliefs as their own?

106. Do you ever feel things would improve if others wouldn't attempt to change your ideas and goals and would let you be?

107. Do other societies and their customs hold any interest for you?

108. Does it bother you to work under the pressure of a deadline or in "peak" season?

109. Do you express your opinions when the subject is of major concern to you?

110. Do you seldom comment either positively or negatively on how others behave?

111. Are there times when you are so absorbed in your work that you don't think about what you're doing or about what is happening around you?

112. Has any person ever unintentionally made you feel bad because you wouldn't reveal your emotions?

113. If you're bored from lack of activity, will you think of something stimulating to break up the monotony?

114. After you've retired, do you go to sleep quickly?

115. Do you like to know what your fellow employees do in their lives?

116. Do you tend to let things lie for a day or so before making up your mind what to do?

117. Does each person expect more consideration for his own ideas and prerogatives than for those of others?

118. Is it always best to cheer for the local teams as opposed to all others?

119. Do you vacillate between being euphoric and despondent?

120. If your first impression of someone is favorable, do you usually keep on regarding him positively, regardless of his later behavior?

121. Have you frequently had superiors who received all the praise for job success and managed to make their subordinates seem to blame for their own errors?

122. Do you normally remain quiet until others address you?

123. Have you ever had to defend someone in a dispute on your team or at your club?

124. When you are in a fine mood, do you mind being around a person who is downhearted?

125. Do you feel certain religious beliefs so absurd that you feel obliged to criticize them?

126. Do you like to forget yourself in fantasies?

127. Is there only one genuine faith or creed for you?

128. Do you frequently find it necessary to sharply reprimand someone who is rude or offensive?

129. Do you have certain special methods that others fail to comprehend or appreciate?

130. At times are you fatigued for no apparent reason?

131. Do you tend to roam or wander about in your sleep?

132. Do you like relating to others and establishing friendships?

133. Do you become enthusiastic about innovations or forward-looking ideas?

134. Do you tend to tell others not to meddle with your concerns and interests?

135. Do you enjoy doing your job in solitude?

136. Would nearly everybody resort to falsehoods to escape a bad situation or "tight spot"?

137. Have you ever regretted not joining in on a venture that ultimately succeeded because you were too skeptical and wary?

138. Can you adopt a new position without difficulty once you've already formed an opinion about something?

139. Do you enjoy being in the middle of things?

140. Are you a prankster who likes to say and do things in jest?

141. Do you appreciate a serious, no-nonsense person?

142. Are most persons stimulating or thought provoking?

143. Have you ever felt a kind of enjoyment at how skillfully some person tricked or fooled you?

144. Does playing games at a party disturb you despite the fact that all the others are participating?

145. Do you have flights of imagination so vivid that you feel as though they were really taking place?

146. When you happen to notice people whom you know only slightly and whom you haven't talked to recently, do you tend to go on your way unless they stop you?

147. Do you experience times when you are going about your daily business but later cannot recall anything about what you did?

148. When several of your friends have fallen out over something, have you ever aided them in coming to terms?

149. Are there matters in your life that you keep exclusively to yourself?

150. Occasionally, do you awaken feeling fatigued and then feel fine once you get up?

151. Has anxiety or apprehension over something ever kept you from sleeping?

152. Is it correct to say that all individuals are actually concerned above all with protecting their own interests?

153. Do you feel sluggish on some occasions and dynamic at other times?

154. Does being around someone who is depressed make your spirits sink, even if you were in a fine mood?

155. Do you like taking sole command of a job and being fully accountable for it?

156. Does it ever happen that an exciting novel makes you feel you're a part of the book?

157. Is somebody who fails to guard his possessions just as much to blame as the person who steals them?

158. Simply as a matter of ethics, would you prevent one person from trying to perpetrate a raw-deal upon another?

159. Can you see matters accurately in your "mind's eye" when you are preparing to act on them?

160. Do you tend to think that life really consists of selecting the best option where all the options are bad?

161. Have you ever used up all your energy reserves by taking on too much?

162. When a person is able to "inspire you" in talking about your job, do you tend to improve?

163. Did any school or university ever dismiss you for academic or other reasons?

164. Do you enjoy a job around others instead of a job by yourself?

165. Has anyone ever taken as his one of your insights or original conceptions?

166. Do you feel in low spirits at times without any apparent reason?

167. At times do you feel so uneasy or jumpy that you feel compelled to move around or take some kind of action?

168. Have you ever been in a touchy, aggravated mood for awhile and then impetuously lost your temper over something minor?

169. Are others frequently so illogical that you can't talk sense to them?

170. Do you sometimes enjoy keeping others guessing about what you will do next?

171. Have you at any time feigned more regret or remorse than you actually felt so that you would not be disciplined for an offense?

172. Are you exasperated when another person persists in showing you how to do your own job?

173. Do you have problems thinking or concentrating if you are in a room where there is a crowd or noise?

174. Would you rather learn something one stage at a time than try to look at it from a broad perspective?

175. Will you actively dispute a matter if a person explicitly opposes you?

176. Have you had any self-defect or imperfection for so long that you've decided to just live with it instead of trying to eliminate it?

177. Do you feel that one should not alter his or her views on some issues?

178. When people make mistakes in conversation in your area of expertise, do you attempt to show them why they are wrong?

179. Do you enjoy making bets?

180. Do you find it thrilling to be in the middle of a great mass of people?

181. Did you ever purposely try to annoy a person you weren't on good terms with?

182. When somebody offers a piece of advice about a project you've completely planned, do you take the advice as willingly as you would have when you were just starting?

183. Is it correct to say that nearly every person thinks above all of his own interests, despite what he may tell others?

184. When you were a child, did anyone ever accuse you of taking something that wasn't yours?

185. Have you ever lost weight because of tension or stress?

186. Are you more insistent and serious-minded than most of the people close to you?

187. Have you ever been forced to request something of somebody when you realized you couldn't return the favor?

188. If the present situation is acceptable to you, do you let it be rather than seek improvements?

189. Do you have trouble with long problems in addition?

190. Do you try to avoid going to parties or dinners when you dislike the hosts?

191. Have others taken notice of your capacities and special gifts and given you the chance to fulfill your potential?

192. Do you become angry quickly and then put your anger aside without much delay?

193. Do you enjoy playing cards for money, rather than just for fun?

194. Have you ever had a spasm or seizure of any kind?

195. Have you ever felt so sure and skilled in your own mind that you were able to perform even elaborate duties?

196. Do you find it difficult to like people whose behavior is wrong?

197. Have you thought many times that those above you were fearful you would equal them in the knowledge of their own jobs?

198. Do you conceal certain goals or plans you have?

199. Are you opposed to customs and practices that differ from the norm even though you can't fault them otherwise?

200. Have you ever repressed your anger so much that you later became ill as a consequence?

201. Do you tend to have only a single confidant with whom you can talk freely?

202. Do you have to combat low spirits or despondency at times?

203. Did you pretend you weren't feeling well in childhood to avoid a responsibility?

204. Do you have something important you would like to do if you had the opportunity?

205. Have you ever taken advantage of a person who has taken advantage of others?

206. Do you ever feel afraid of being enclosed in a small area?

207. Do you frequently observe that others are unable to tolerate advice aimed at helping them to improve?

208. Do you feel irritated if you turn down a chance because you're too cautious and then another person makes a windfall off your opportunity?

209. Do you find that emotional speeches can deeply move you?

210. If someone made a mistake in conversation, would you point out his error?

211. Do you get more out of watching sports when you wager on the outcome?

212. Does it disturb you to stop a task for something else even if the interruption is only temporary?

213. Did you ever steal any small items in your childhood?

214. Is your concentration readily disturbed by talking or ordinary sounds?

215. Have you ever put aside a friendship so that you could better accomplish your own goals?

216. Did you ever unintentionally provoke a dispute among your friends as a result of an unthinking remark?

217. Do you enjoy being a member of groups and associations?

218. Do you dislike certain people to the extent that you rejoice if they suffer misfortunes?

219. Do you have difficulty keeping to your beliefs?

220. Is your life generally stable, with little change or vacillation?

221. Are you capable of accepting negative remarks if they're intended to help you?

222. Do you prefer repetitive, meticulous work over jobs that involve different duties and much change?

223. Do you believe someone should always be honest and straightforward?

224. Do you suffer serious nervous headaches or have intense pain in the head region?

225. Do you devote your attention to numerous hobbies instead of concentrating on a single leisure activity?

226. Have you ever suffered an emotional collapse of any kind?

227. Do you feel nervous and queasy looking down from tall buildings or great elevations?

228. In your adulthood, has any person bothered you to the point that you've had to physically attack that person?

229. Do you think complete honesty is the best policy if you are in a jam?

230. Do you disregard or forget your possessions with the result that you don't take full advantage of them?

231. Are most people ultimately underhanded and deceptive when they see their chance?

232. When something favorable happens to you, do you feel just as good about it if it's a secret as when you can talk about it?

233. Have you ever thought that a person was attempting to use you despite the fact that you lacked solid proof of his intentions?

234. When you feel particularly sharp and alert, does that give you a quiet, strong feeling of self-confidence?

235. Have you ever accepted work where concentrating on the small points was the only important aspect of the job?

236. Can you hold a person responsible who uses someone when the second person has almost invited the other to exploit him?

237. When a thrilling or stirring event occurs, does it occasionally lift you out of the doldrums?

238. Has your weight ever gone down as a result of your worrying over difficulties?

239. Do you think of yourself as tense or excitable?

240. Do you tend to be uncomfortably aware of how others perceive you?

241. When you start to work somewhere, do you like to discover those people whom you'll need to know to improve your position?

242. Do you prefer not to worry about small points or particulars?

243. If something is a common or universal practice, does that indicate you will do well to follow it most of the time?

244. Do you have trouble putting money aside to use in the future?

245. Do you frequently seek out others to find out what you should do?

246. Do you have the feeling at times that you know exactly what to do and can decide quickly without effort?

247. When younger, did you sometimes skip a day at school?

248. Do your worst problems involve solving your own internal conflicts?

249. Do you have any personal methods of keeping your temper, such as holding your breath or counting to 10?

250. If you could do well either way, would you want to work at several things at once rather than finish one job and then go to the next until you were through?

251. Do you believe that a large number of people will be untruthful when deception will help their cause?

252. Did you ever think that others were discussing you in your absence?

253. Do you enjoy relating anecdotes and speaking in jest?

254. Have you ever poked fun at a particular religious faith and then discovered that someone listening to you was of that faith?

255. If a rumor or story is going around in your group of friends, do you feel everyone learns of it before you?

256. Do sounds wake you up easily?

257. Do you believe that most people aren't crooked or untruthful because the thought of being apprehended or found out deters them?

258. At times do you fail to recognize that you are really fatigued until after you take a break?

259. In grammar school were you ordered to report to the principal's office every once in a while because of misconduct?

260. Is your sleep seldom, if ever, interrupted by suddenly waking up?

261. Are you frequently amazed that the authorities in your field have so little knowledge?

262. Are you constantly on the lookout for methods to improve or to become more efficient?

263. Do you take a general overview and then let the small points take care of themselves as you proceed?

264. Are you troubled by medical disorders or ailments more than most people?

265. Do you elaborately prepare for even the smallest fine points before beginning something?

266. Do you enjoy "clowning around" with friends and carrying out pranks on each other?

267. Will you persist in something you believe in down to the last minute, even though you can't win?

268. Have you ever been scared about matters that you later recognized were of no consequence?

269. Is it hard for you to go to sleep when you're exhilarated or elated?

270. Do your preparations for the future frequently become so difficult that you must abandon them?

271. Are you prone to fainting spells or blackouts?

272. Have you ever become so infuriated that you lashed out with words or actions that you later wished you could take back?

273. Are you irresolute or undetermined?

274. Do your emotional attitudes about most persons tend to be either very negative or very positive?

275. Have you ever experienced a time when you were almost totally unnerved and restless, with only a bare hold on yourself?

276. Are there times when you are queasy or sick to your stomach?

277. Have you frequently altered your plans about what you wanted to do with your life?

278. Were you often reprimanded or disciplined when you had done something wrong?

279. Have you ever had a sudden insight that altered your life-style and still affects you today?

280. Have you ever yearned to have the leisure and financial resources to keep up with such sports as polo, yachting, boxing, and car racing?

281. Do you find it difficult to comprehend why people act in ways that don't seem right?

282. Do you like being with lively, vivacious people?

283. Do you feel sorry for the oppressed and unfortunate?

284. Have you ever been trapped in a bad situation because a person you had faith in deceived you?

285. Are you immobilized at times by issues because you have to look at them from so many angles?

286. Do you think about a tactic before following through on it, as a general rule?

287. Do you know people who are frightened of you?

288. Do you enjoy a variety of tasks in a job?

289. At a social gathering do you prefer to stay with one person instead of mingling with others?

290. Are there times when, for no tangible reason, you don't trust yourself or have confidence in yourself?

291. Do you have only a very select group of friends in whom you confide when you have problems?

292. Can you forget about setbacks and go about your business optimistically?

293. Do you ever make a purchase when you actually don't like the product and have no need for it?

294. Do you regard your opinion as final once you've reached it?

295. Have you ever been convinced that others were gossiping about you, despite your lack of evidence to prove it?

296. Do you object when your friends make fun of you, even in jest?

297. In your youth, were you a member of any close-knit groups?

298. Are you more troubled and apprehensive at certain times than at others?

299. Have you ever stayed away from a person for fear you would make a comment or take an action you would later regret?

300. If a criminal is very clever, have you ever wished that he could escape detection?

301. Has any person ever impeded your progress in your profession or hindered your promotion?

302. Are you fond of reading about the experiences of people who visit foreign lands?

303. Do you permit yourself just a small number of friendships?

304. Do you feel isolated at times despite being in a large group?

305. Have you found on a number of occasions that you've accomplished more work than you initially thought possible?

306. Are you sometimes faced by such difficult, intricate problems that you are nearly unable to reach a decision?

307. Do you banish your cares and problems when you are with gregarious, outgoing friends?

308. Have you upset others because you said something without thinking?

309. Does it bother you when you are forced to revise or revamp your strategy in the middle of acting?

310. Do you go through periods when you're not as mentally alert as you are normally?

311. Do you think it's always wise not to say anything when you are in a difficult predicament?

312. Do you find it necessary at times to rest in the daytime even when you're not feeling ill?

313. Are others jealous of you because you frequently have original, productive thoughts before they do?

314. In your childhood did you ever pretend to be ill or hurt?

315. Do you have such bad dreams that you occasionally cry out in your sleep and disturb others?

316. Are you ever fearful that you won't have a single friend?

317. Do you enjoy a large variety of activities for entertainment?

318. Have you ever pretended to be in poor health so that you could keep out of difficulties?

319. Do you believe that others really dislike doing a favor for someone, although they will for purposes of image?

320. Do you neglect small points in your work so that you can retain the key ideas?

320 QUESTIONNAIRE–Answer Sheet *(Please Print)*

Last Name _____ M.I. _____ First _____

Social Security Number _____ Date _____

Company Sponsoring this Exercise _____

Person _____ Title _____

Company Address _____

City _____ State _____ Zip Code _____

Y N		Y N		Y N		Y N		Y N		Y N		Y N		Y N		Y N
1		41		81		121		161		201		241		281	
2		42		82		122		162		202		242		282	
3		43		83		123		163		203		243		283	
4		44		84		124		164		204		244		284	
5		45		85		125		165		205		245		285	
6		46		86		126		166		206		246		286	
7		47		87		127		167		207		247		287	
8		48		88		128		168		208		248		288	
9		49		89		129		169		209		249		289	
10		50		90		130		170		210		250		290	
11		51		91		131		171		211		251		291	
12		52		92		132		172		212		252		292	
13		53		93		133		173		213		253		293	
14		54		94		134		174		214		254		294	
15		55		95		135		175		215		255		295	
16		56		96		136		176		216		256		296	
17		57		97		137		177		217		257		297	
18		58		98		138		178		218		258		298	
19		59		99		139		179		219		259		299	
20		60		100		140		180		220		260		300	
21		61		101		141		181		221		261		301	
22		62		102		142		182		222		262		302	
23		63		103		143		183		223		263		303	
24		64		104		144		184		224		264		304	
25		65		105		145		185		225		265		305	
26		66		106		146		186		226		266		306	
27		67		107		147		187		227		267		307	
28		68		108		148		188		228		268		308	
29		69		109		149		189		229		269		309	
30		70		110		150		190		230		270		310	
31		71		111		151		191		231		271		311	
32		72		112		152		192		232		272		312	
33		73		113		153		193		233		273		313	
34		74		114		154		194		234		274		314	
35		75		115		155		195		235		275		315	
36		76		116		156		196		236		276		316	
37		77		117		157		197		237		277		317	
38		78		118		158		198		238		278		318	
39		79		119		159		199		239		279		319	
40		80		120		160		200		240		280		320	

Index

Accomplishments, and behavior traits, 50

Achiever, personal characteristics of, 132–33

Active person, 15–17; adaptability of, 141; ambitions of, 55; awards/honors of, 42; and communication, 145; company attitude of, 46; compared to entrepreneur, 15; compared to overachiever, 15; delegation by, 126; description of, 17; drive of, 115, 130, 131; education financing by, 43; and emotions, 17; establishing rapport with, 105; extracurricular activities of, 41, 111; favorite school subjects of, 36; and favorite supervisor, 48; future job/salary goals of, 47; and hardest supervisor, 49; and human relationships, 15–17; and intelligence, 33–34; and interest in future school courses, 38; interviewing style of, 87; and judgment/decisiveness, 123; and persuasiveness, 116, 142–43; and planning/ organizing, 117; position capability of, 50; positions preferred by, 43; ranking of candidate for, 76; ranking of interviewer for, 80; response to beginning of interview process, 106; and risk taking, 124; self-description by, 112–13; and self-esteem trait, 135; self-image of, 54; sentence completions by, 56–65; and significant teachers, 39, 40; and spare time activities, 51; and stress tolerance trait, 139; troublesome courses for, 37; values and motivation of, 35; work history of, 109–10; work-related group membership of, 52

Adaptability: in conjunction with behavior trait/type, 140–42; definition of, 114, 139; and sensitivity, 140

Aggressive person, 22–25; and adaptability, 141; ambitions of, 55, 56; comparison with sensitized person, 22–23; degree of, 24; and delegation, 127; description of, 25; drive of, 115, 130–31; educational experiences of, 108; education financing by, 43; establishing rapport with, 105; extracurricular activities of, 41, 111; favorite school subjects of, 36; and favorite supervisor, 48, 49; future job/salary goals of, 47; and insecurity, 23–24; interviewing style of, 87–88; job history of, 44; and judgment/decisiveness, 123; and leadership, 24; and least favorite job, 45; and persuasiveness, 116, 143; and planning/organizing, 119; position capability of, 50; ranking of in-

About the Author

JAMES B. WEITZUL, Ph.D., is a partner in the consulting firm of Banks & Weitzul. During his professional career he has worked for the Rand Corporation and Rohrer Hibler and Replogle. He is a frequent contributor to business journals in areas of Managerial Psychology, consults with various organizations in the areas of personnel selection and organizational design, and serves on the Board of Directors of Corporations. He is currently working on his second book, which deals with revitalizing an organization's sales force.